New Course

New Course

Pitman New Era Shorthand

PITMAN PUBLISHING LIMITED
128 Long Acre, London WC2E 9AN

Associated Companies
Pitman Publishing Pty Ltd, Melbourne
Pitman Publishing New Zealand Ltd, Wellington

Decimalized edition 1978

Reprinted 1979, 1981, 1982, 1983 (twice), 1984

Text set in 9/10pt Times New Roman
Printed and bound in Great Britain
at The Pitman Press, Bath

ISBN 0 273 42231 6

PREFACE

ISAAC PITMAN published the first edition of his shorthand system in 1837. He spent half a century improving it, and the great work has since been continued by several generations of expert writers and teachers.

Millions have used this system as a means of earning a livelihood, and today, throughout the world, wherever accurate and immediately legible recording of spoken English is required, in Parliaments and Congresses, in the Courts of Justice, and in offices of every size and sort, there is Pitman Shorthand, doing what no machine can so effectively reproduce, the whole speech and nothing but the speech (with whatever helpful notes the intelligent recorder may choose to append to the speech), in a form that can be read like a book as soon as it is written or ten years afterwards. No system has been tested for so long or by so many writers of such a wide diversity of natural aptitude; and no system has won so high a reputation on the testing ground of experience.

DISTINCTIVE FEATURES OF THE SYSTEM

Isaac Pitman devised his system after a profound and epoch-making study of the phonetic structure of the English language. The system is a result of his scientific analysis. Systems before Pitman, and even some systems in use today, could achieve speed only through the laborious memorization of hundreds of special forms and arbitrary abbreviations. In Pitman Shorthand, speed and facility of writing and safety of reading are achieved by following a coherent and comprehensive scheme: each individual sound has its sign, and sounds of the same family have signs with an appropriate family likeness, so that, after a little practice, the signs seem to produce themselves like snapshots from the sounds, and the sounds themselves seem to speak from the written page.

Handwriting Motion Inadequate. The consonants of the language are represented by a series of simple strokes, selected to provide the most facile joinings with one another. Because these strokes do not follow the slope of ordinary longhand writing, they can be formed with complete distinctiveness when they are joined together and written with great speed. The purpose of shorthand is to represent letters as briefly and as distinctively as possible. *The adoption of a uniform slope in a shorthand system would result in a confusing similarity*

iii

of consonants, and the hand of the writer would be retarded because of the necessity for careful and laborious representation of fine distinctions.

Pairing of Consonants. In certain cases consonants are paired because of their similarity of sound. The first consonant in the pair is pronounced lightly (as "S") and is unvoiced, and the second consonant in the pair is the corresponding heavy sound (as "Z") and is voiced. The same stroke is used for both consonants, but for the first consonant a light stroke is written, and the second stroke of the pair is written with a slight pressure of the pen. *This avoids the necessity of employing different strokes to represent similarly sounded consonants.* If, for instance, half- and double-length strokes were used to represent these pairs, valuable shorthand abbreviating material would be lost, which in Pitman Shorthand is used to represent the addition of letters and even whole syllables. *The use of this device thus saves time and labour for the shorthand writer and involves no extra penmanship.*

Elimination of Vowel Signs. Words are represented by a complete shorthand outline of their consonants. Short forms are provided for common words. Circles, loops and hooks are used for the representation of frequently occurring and natural combinations of consonants in English words. In the application of this abbreviating material the presence or absence of a vowel is indicated, and it is unnecessary to write signs for the vowel sounds. *Here again the shorthand writer is saved much time and labour.* A series of disjoined vowel signs is provided for insertion where necessary, such as in isolated words, or proper names.

Position Writing. Position writing is a simple and effective device for the indication of vowels. Writing a word above, on, or through the line, according to its first vowel sound, *is another means of expressing sound without actual writing, and it is a device highly prized by the fastest writers.* Generations of the best writers in the world have proved that the most effective means of securing compact, swift and legible shorthand outlines is through complete representation of the consonants, and that the insertion of the vowel signs is not ordinarily necessary.

Summary. In Pitman Shorthand the amount of actual writing has been reduced to a minimum because of the scientific use of the stenographic abbreviating material. Circles, loops, hooks, halving and doubling are devices used for the representation of syllables, and not for the formation of an alphabet. An adequate skill in shorthand writing is developed through the application of the abbreviating principles of the system. These devices are few in number, and they are easily understood and applied.

FEATURES OF THE BOOK

This book presents the principles of Pitman Shorthand in a logical arrangement. The principles are stated briefly and simply, and each statement is followed by an adequate amount of application. The work of the teacher is made easier by dividing the principles into small units of construction.

An unusual feature of the book is the wealth of drill material provided for each unit of instruction. The amount of this material is more than that appearing in any shorthand textbook previously issued. The exercises have been so compiled that they are similar in subject matter to the material dictated to students in later stages of the study of the subject. The development of skill in reading and writing these exercises is therefore of great importance, for they provide practice as valuable to the student as the dictation he will receive when the principles have been completed. Realization of this will encourage the student and will stimulate rapid progress. The exercises provide a cumulative review of the principles and of the short forms.

In the application of the principles a vocabulary of the two thousand commonest words has been used. Less frequently occurring words are used occasionally, however, to provide additional illustrations and to demonstrate in the exercises the application of a principle to similar words. These additional words are always well within the average student's vocabulary.

Most of the exercises are in shorthand. Reading correct shorthand is invaluable to the student, and the reading approach makes it possible to prevent students from writing or seeing incorrectly written outlines, and in this way assists them to write accurately from the start. The shorthand exercises are also useful for home preparation and from Chapter IX onwards longhand exercise or dictation material is included.

Dictation is always interesting to the student, and teachers will find *Graded Dictation Studies* of great use to them when used side by side with the NEW COURSE. In this book there is a wealth of dictation material arranged so as to correspond accurately with the chapters of the NEW COURSE and at the same time progressively graded by word-frequency. Complete practice for dictation purposes is also given in the whole vocabulary of each chapter of the NEW COURSE, including short forms, phrases and word lists.

The very frequently used words expressed in shorthand by some logical principle of abbreviation are introduced in their appropriate places in the text and are also given in three alphabetically arranged lists at the end of the volume. The first list gives those short forms that are included in the text and these all come within the two thousand commonest words. The second list gives additional short forms occurring in the first ten thousand commonest words, and the third list a few others which do not occur in the ten thousand commonest words. It will be noticed that for all ordinary purposes the first list is adequate and in fact represents between 50 and 60 per cent of average matter.

Reference can be made to the wide selection of Pitman shorthand books which will be most useful for consolidating and expanding the principles by different approaches, supplying also abundant material for reading and dictation.

Much dictation material is available in the *Shorthand Speed Development* series. These books and the *New Course* itself are provided with supporting sound-tapes.

Shorthand material appears each month in the Pitman periodical *Memo*.

CONTENTS

INTRODUCTION

SHORTHAND is the art of representing spoken sounds by written signs. Pitman Shorthand provides a way of representing every sound heard in English words.

Ordinary longhand spelling is seldom phonetic. Pitman Shorthand is phonetic; that is, words are generally written as they are sounded and not according to ordinary longhand spelling. With certain exceptions no signs are used that are not wanted to represent the sound.

The following illustrations show how to think of the words when writing shorthand—

palm is *p-ah-m*	*wrought* is *r-aw-t*
pale is *p-ay-l*	*coal* is *k-oh-l*
key is *k-ee*	*tomb* is *t-oo-m*

With the exception of *worsted* (the woollen material) and a few proper names, e.g. *Worcester*, if an R appears in the spelling of a word it always appears in the shorthand. Words that include a "silent R" in some pronunciations of English are thus made much easier to read, e.g. *iron, park*.

The shorthand characters should be made as neatly and as accurately as possible. The size of the shorthand strokes in this book is a good standard to adopt in your own writing. The signs join readily with one another and they can be written with great speed when practised sufficiently. Resist the temptation to sacrifice accurate formation for speed. Speed in writing will naturally follow the practice of neat and accurate writing.

CHAPTER 1

1. The First Six Consonants

The sounds heard in English words are, in Pitman Shorthand divided into—

Twenty-four Consonants   Twelve Vowels   Four Diphthongs

A shorthand sign is provided for each of these sounds.

The first six consonants are represented by straight strokes written downward—

Letter	Sign	Name	As in
P		pee	pay, ape, up
B		bee	bay, Abe, be
T		tee	Tay, ate, it
D		dee	day, aid, do
CH		chay	chest, etch, which
J		jay	jest, edge, age

The arrows indicate the direction in which the strokes are written. They are never written in any other direction.

NOTE: These consonants form pairs: *p* and *b*, *t* and *d*, *ch* and *j*. In each pair a *light* sound is represented by a *light* stroke, and a corresponding *heavy* sound is represented by a *heavier* stroke.

2. Vowel *ā*

Vowels are represented by dots and dashes written alongside the consonant strokes. When a vowel comes *before* a consonant, it is placed *before* the stroke (left side); when a vowel comes *after* a consonant, it is placed *after* the stroke (right side).

1

The long vowel *ā* is represented by a heavy dot—

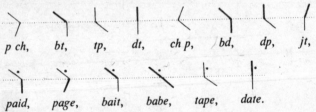

ape,   pay,   Abe,   bay,   aid,   day,   age.

Write the consonant stroke first and then place the vowel sign. Two light dashes underneath an outline indicate that the word represented begins with a capital letter.

> NOTE: There are three places alongside a stroke in which vowels may be written—beginning, middle, and end, or first, second, and third place. The dot for long *ā* is written in the middle place, and it is therefore called a "second-place vowel."

3. Joining of Consonants

Consonants are joined without lifting the pen, as in longhand. Begin the second where the first ends, and write the stroke in its proper direction. Note that the first stroke rests on the line.

p ch,   bt,   tp,   dt,   ch p,   bd,   dp,   jt,

paid,   page,   bait,   babe,   tape,   date.

4. Vowel *ĕ*

Short *ĕ* is represented by a light dot, and is a second-place vowel—

etch,   edge,   bet,   pep,   Ted,   debt,   jet.

NOTE: The first stroke rests on the line. Write the consonant outline first, and then place the vowel sign.

5. Short Forms for Common Words

A few very frequently used words, such as *be, it, the, to,* are expressed in shorthand by a single sign. These short forms promote speedy writing, and they should be thoroughly memorized—

be,   it,   do,   which,   the,   to,   two or too,   but,   who.

6. Phrasing

As an aid to rapid writing, shorthand words may often be joined. This is called phrasing. Outlines should be phrased only when they join easily and naturally, as shown in the examples throughout this textbook. The first word in a phrase is written in its normal position—

to do,   *but which.*

A small tick *at the end* of a word represents *the*. The tick is written either upward or downward, whichever forms the sharper angle but, whether written upward or downward, its angle to the line of writing is always the same—

to the, be the, do the, which the, pay the, paid the.

7. Punctuation

The following special punctuation marks are used in shorthand—

X or ɣ   ?   !   =   ⌐   { }

full stop,   question,   exclamation,   hyphen,   dash,   parenthesis.

Other signs are written as in longhand.

Exercise 1

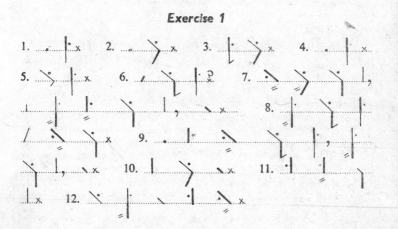

CHAPTER II

8. The Second Group of Consonants

The next four pairs of consonants are curves, and they are written downward—

Letter	Sign	Name	As in	Short Form for
F	⅄	ef	few, safe, for	
V	⅄	vee	view, save, have	have ⌣
TH	⅄(	ith	*th*igh, ba*th*, *th*ink	think (
TH	⅄(	thee	**th**y, ba**th**e, **th**em	them (
S	⅄)	ess	seal, ice, us	
Z	⅄)	zee	zeal, eyes, was	was)
SH	⅄	ish	she, wish, shall	shall)
ZH	⅄	zhee	measure, treasure, usual	usual/ly)

(a) *they,* *say,* *fade,* *faith,* *shape,* *bathe,* *shade.*

(b) *fed,* *fetch,* *death,* *shed,* *essay.*

9. Vowels ō and ŭ

Long ō is represented by a heavy dash, and is a second-place vowel—

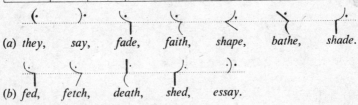

toe, *oat,* *bow,* *Joe,* *foe,* *oath,* *so,* *owes,*

show, *showed,* *boat,* *both,* *vote.*

4

Short *ŭ* is represented by a light dash, and is a second-place vowel—

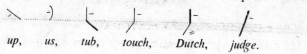

up,   us,   tub,   touch,   Dutch,   judge.

Exercise 2

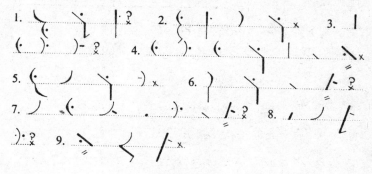

Exercise 3

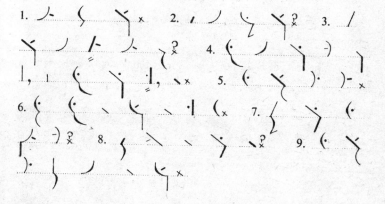

CHAPTER III

10. The Next Eight Consonants

The next eight consonants are all written forward. They are all light strokes except *g* and *ng*—

Letter	Sign	Name	As in	Short Form for
K		kay	cane, leak, come	*come* _____
G		gay	gain, league, give	*give* or *given* _____
M		em	may, seem, him	*him* _____
N		en	nay, seen, no	
NG		ing	long, sing, thing	*thing* _____
L		el	lay, coal, will	*lord* _____
W		way	weigh, aware, we	*we* _____
Y		yay	youth, yellow, yes	

When a vowel comes *before* a horizontal stroke it is written *above* the stroke; when a vowel comes *after* a horizontal stroke it is written *below* the stroke.

(a) ache, egg, gay, keg, cake, aim, may, make, came, game, gum, comb, no, know, name, neck.

(b) ail, lay, laid, led, lake, delay, low, load, below, love, luck, lung, coal, goal, mail.

(c) way, weigh, woe, web, wed, wedge, yoke, yellow.

6

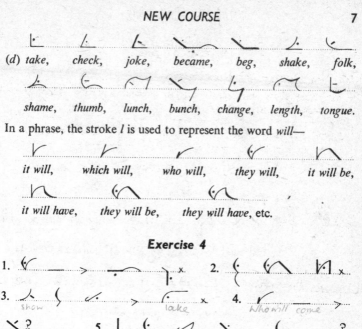

(d) *take, check, joke, became, beg, shake, folk,*

shame, thumb, lunch, bunch, change, length, tongue.

In a phrase, the stroke *l* is used to represent the word *will*—

it will, which will, who will, they will, it will be,

it will have, they will be, they will have, etc.

Exercise 4

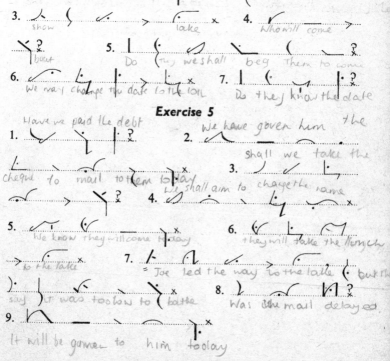

1. ____ Sh...

2. ____

3. show ____ lake

4. Whom will come

5. Do they we shall beg them to come
   bout

6. We may change the date later on

7. Do they know the date

Exercise 5

1. Have we paid the debt

2. We have given him the

3. cheque to mail to them today
   shall we take the

4. We shall aim to change the name

5. We know they will come today

6. they will take the lunch

7. to the table
   = Joe led the way to the table (but the

8. say) it was too low to (battle
   Was the mail delayed

9. It will be given to him today

Exercise 6

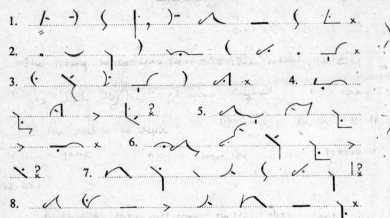

CHAPTER IV

11. First-place Vowels

The next four vowels are written in the *first* place, that is, at the beginning of a stroke. When the *first* vowel in a word is a *first-place* vowel, the outline is written in *first* position, that is, the first downstroke or upstroke in the outline is written *above* the line. First-position outlines consisting of horizontal strokes are written above the line.

(*a*) Long *ah* is represented by a heavy dot—

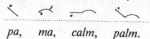

pa,   ma,   calm,   palm.

(*b*) Short *ă* is represented by a light dot—

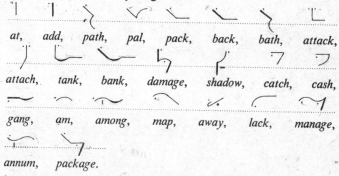

at,   add,   path,   pal,   pack,   back,   bath,   attack,

attach,   tank,   bank,   damage,   shadow,   catch,   cash,

gang,   am,   among,   map,   away,   lack,   manage,

annum,   package.

(*c*) Long *aw* is represented by a heavy dash—

saw,   paw,   ball,   bought,   talk,   tall,   auto,   chalk,

jaw,   law.

(*d*) Short *ŏ* is represented by a light dash—

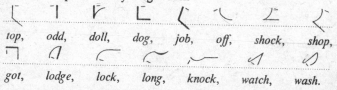

top,   odd,   doll,   dog,   job,   off,   shock,   shop,

got,   lodge,   lock,   long,   knock,   watch,   wash.

SHORT FORMS

⌣ *for*, · *a or an*, ＼ *of*, ˡ *on*, ˡ *had*.

Phrases—

⌣ *on the*, ⌐ *but the* (the signs for *on* and *but* slightly slanted).

Exercise 7

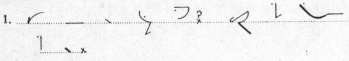

1. [shorthand outlines]

2. [shorthand outlines]

3. [shorthand outlines]

4. [shorthand outlines]

5. [shorthand outlines]

6. [shorthand outlines]

7. [shorthand outlines]
Bob owes the debt. But the watch was paid for on the loan.

8. [shorthand outlines]
thinks chalk may damage the bag. No, it will come off. Wash it off.

9. [shorthand outlines]
Ask Paul to attach the tag to the top of the bag.

10. [shorthand outlines]
We shall check the damage to the boat.

Exercise 8

1.

2.

3.

4.

5.

6.

7.

8.

9.

10.

12. Second Position

When a *second-place* vowel is the *first* vowel in a word, the outline is written in *second* position, that is, the first downstroke or upstroke rests on the line—

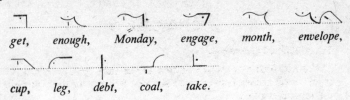

get, enough, Monday, engage, month, envelope,

cup, leg, debt, coal, take.

Exercise 9

1.

2.

3.

4.

5.

6.

7.

8.

9.

10.

CHAPTER V

13. Third-place Vowels

The last four vowels are written in the third place. When a third-place vowel comes between two strokes, it is put in third place before the second stroke.

When a third-place vowel is the first vowel in a word, the outline is written in third position, that is, the first downstroke or upstroke is written through the line.

(*a*) Long *ē* is represented by a heavy dot—

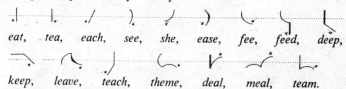

eat, tea, each, see, she, ease, fee, feed, deep, keep, leave, teach, theme, deal, meal, team.

(*b*) Short *ĭ* is represented by a light dot—

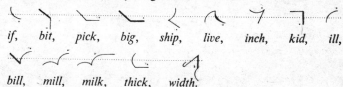

if, bit, pick, big, ship, live, inch, kid, ill, bill, mill, milk, thick, width.

(*c*) Long *ōō* is represented by a heavy dash—

chew, shoe, food, move, youth, tool, pool, cool, tooth.

(*d*) Short *ŏŏ* is represented by a light dash—

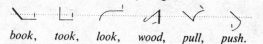

book, took, look, wood, pull, push.

NOTE: The sound of *y* at the end of a word is represented by the light dot *ĭ*.

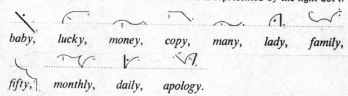

baby, lucky, money, copy, many, lady, family, fifty, monthly, daily, apology.

13

Where an outline consists only of horizontal strokes and the first vowel is a third-position vowel, the outline is written *on* the line—

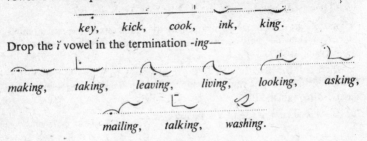

key, kick, cook, ink, king.

Drop the ĭ vowel in the termination *-ing*—

making, taking, leaving, living, looking, asking,

mailing, talking, washing.

SHORT FORMS

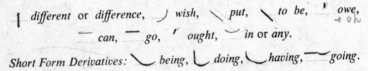

different or *difference*, *wish*, *put*, *to be*, *owe*, *can*, *go*, *ought*, *in* or *any*.

Short Form Derivatives: *being*, *doing*, *having*, *going*.

Exercise 10

7.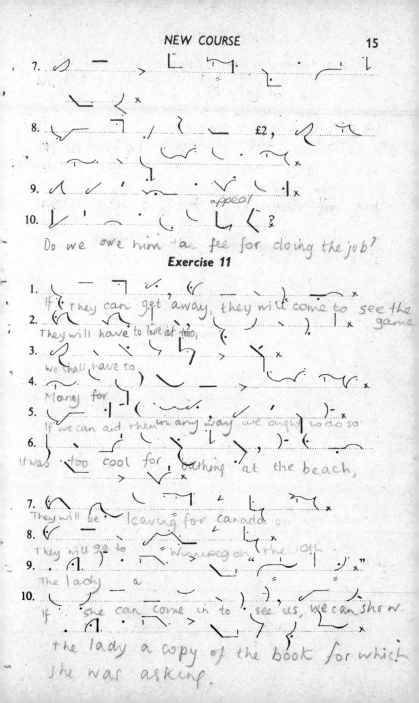
We,

8. £2,

9.
appeal

10.
Do we owe him a fee for doing the job?

Exercise 11

1. If they can get away, they will come to see the game

2. They will have to live at two,

3. We shall have to

4. Money for

5. If we can aid them in any way we ought to do so

6. It was too cool for bathing at the beach,

7. They will be leaving for Canada on

8. They will go to Winnipeg on the 10th

9. The lady — a

10. If she can come in to see us, we can show
the lady a copy of the book for which
she was asking.

Exercise 12

1. We shall be lucky if we get any money for doing the job.

2. Maybe the lunch can be given on a different day.

3. A talk was to be given on the trip. Feeding the family.

4. Eva was talking of going to _____ in May.

5. If they wish to make any money they will have to do the job in a different way.

6. The wood was too thick. It was an inch in width so we had to ship it back.

7. We wish to know if it will make any difference to them if we ship the load of coal today.

8. The change may be put into effect in May.

9. We have no wish to make a change which will effect so many but they have a different way of looking at it.

10. If we can think of any way of doing the thing in a different way, we shall ask them to come in to see us.

CHAPTER VI

14. Two Forms for R

Letter	Sign	Name	As in
R	↗	ray	raw, reach, carry
	↘	ar	car, air, dare

When *r* begins a word use ╱ as in—

red, raw, road, route, rug, rush, ring, reach, ready,

readily, retail, wrong, range, rank, relief, relieve.

When a word begins with the combination "*vowel-r*" use ⌒ as in—

air, arm, or, ear, early, army.

SHORT FORMS

(up) are, (up) our or hour, (up) and, (up) should.

NOTE: *Chay and Ray*: These strokes are somewhat similar, but they are different in slope and in the direction in which they are written. *Chay* is always written downward at a small angle from the vertical.

Ray is always written upward at a small angle from the horizontal.

For the inclusion of consonant *r* in shorthand writing, see Introduction, p. viii.

Exercise 13

1.

To our relief, they came early

2.

We are ... to day and we should reach

Winnipeg in a day or two.

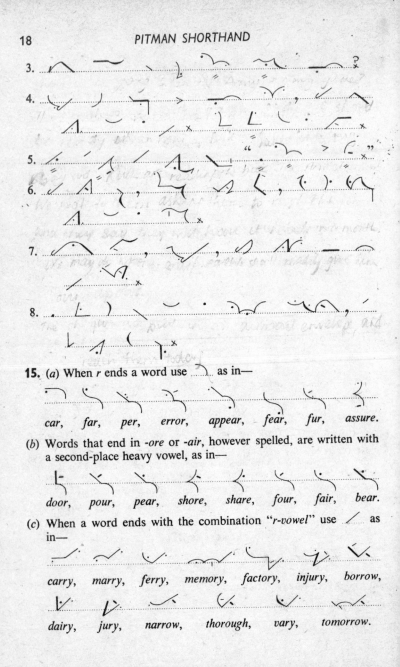

3.

4.

5.

6.

7.

8.

15. (*a*) When *r* ends a word use ⌒ as in—

car,   far,   per,   error,   appear,   fear,   fur,   assure.

(*b*) Words that end in *-ore* or *-air*, however spelled, are written with a second-place heavy vowel, as in—

door,   pour,   pear,   shore,   share,   four,   fair,   bear.

(*c*) When a word ends with the combination "*r-vowel*" use ╱ as in—

carry,   marry,   ferry,   memory,   factory,   injury,   borrow,

dairy,   jury,   narrow,   thorough,   vary,   tomorrow.

SHORT FORMS

⟍ *your,* ⟋ *year,* ⟩ *whose,* ⟨ *large,* ⟨ *thank* or *thanked.*

NOTE: In the phrase "*to go*" ⟍⟋ the vowel is inserted.

Exercise 14

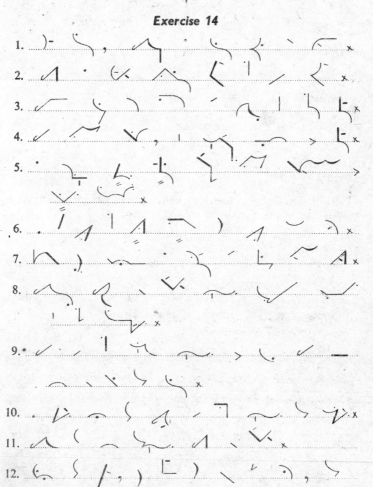

16. In order to avoid awkward joinings *r* is written—

EXCEPTIONS – VOWEL INDICATION RULES ignored here.

(*a*) Downward before *m*—

room,   Rome,   remedy,   form,   firm,   alarm,   remove.

(*b*) Upward before *t, d, ch, j* and *th*—

errata,   arid,   arch,   urge,   earth.

(*c*) Upward after a straight upstroke—

rear,   rare,   roar,   aware,   career,   lawyer.

NOTE: Usually it is better to write upward *r* in the middle of a word—

March,   party,   park,   forty,   authority,   charge,   garage,

fourth,   mark,   parade,   thoroughly.

- Down 'r'

Exercise 15

1. *charge for the rug was put on your March bill*

2. *We wish to remove any fear they may have, and
we shall urge them to engage a lawyer.*

3. *May we take Polly and Jack to see the parade
on the fourth of March.*

4.

We shall make up a party and have lunch at the cake shop.

5.

We are making a tour of Italy in March.

6.

Our party should be in Rome on the 4th of the

7.

We shall get back to Canada in May. month

8.

The usual charge for parking the car at the garage-wash! £1

9.

We saw the copy of the rare book in the shop window.

10.

It should pay the farmer to go on the air daily.

11.

Paul King was put in charge of the factory. early in March.

12.

We can put a mark in red at the bottom of each page we check

Exercise 16

1.

Mary and Jack are to be married early in March

2.

We wish to go to the wedding, but they may be married in Rome and it will be too far away.

3.

We shall ask the lawyer to talk for an hour.

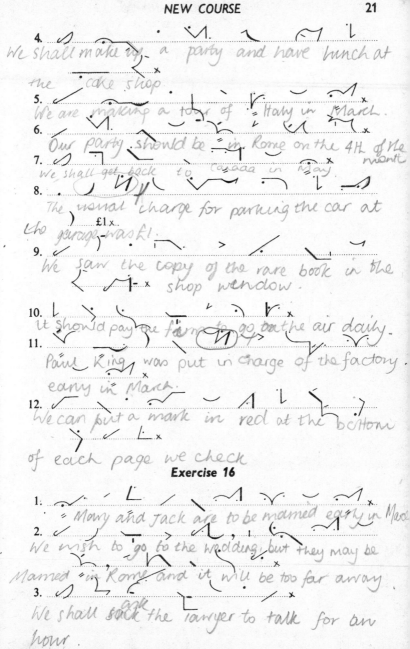

4. They will take a lorry load of coal to the shop today or tomorrow

5. Wrap the package and mail it today. We think we ought to insure the package.

6. We have given them no authority to change the policy of the firm.

7. We get our milk at the dairy farm, and we usually pay our bill monthly.

8. The living room was at the rear of the shop

9. The door was too narrow, and we had to remove it to get the large package into the room.

10. Mary, whose memory was poor, read a different page of the book each day.

11. We can change the colour of the fur wrap today and the lady may come in for it tomorrow.

CHAPTER VII

17. Diphthongs

The four double vowels used in Pitman's Shorthand are *i*, *oi*, *ow*, and *u*, as heard in the words *I enjoy Gow's music*.

(*a*) The diphthong *i* is represented by a small angular mark written as shown, in the first vowel place—

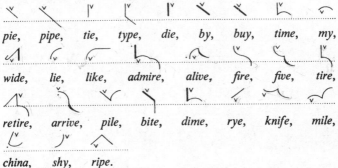

pie,   pipe,   tie,   type,   die,   by,   buy,   time,   my,

wide,   lie,   like,   admire,   alive,   fire,   five,   tire,

retire,   arrive,   pile,   bite,   dime,   rye,   knife,   mile,

china,   shy,   ripe.

(*b*) The diphthong *oi* is written as shown, in the first vowel place—

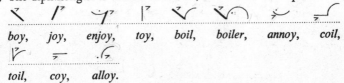

boy,   joy,   enjoy,   toy,   boil,   boiler,   annoy,   coil,

toil,   coy,   alloy.

(*c*) The diphthong *ow* is written as shown, in the third vowel place—

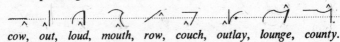

cow,   out,   loud,   mouth,   row,   couch,   outlay,   lounge,   county.

(*d*) The diphthong *u* is represented by a small semicircle written in the third vowel place—

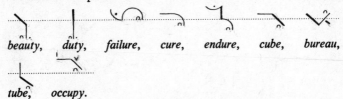

beauty,   duty,   failure,   cure,   endure,   cube,   bureau,

tube,   occupy.

SHORT FORMS

I or eye, how, why, beyond, you, with, when, what, would, me, owing. language

Exercise 17

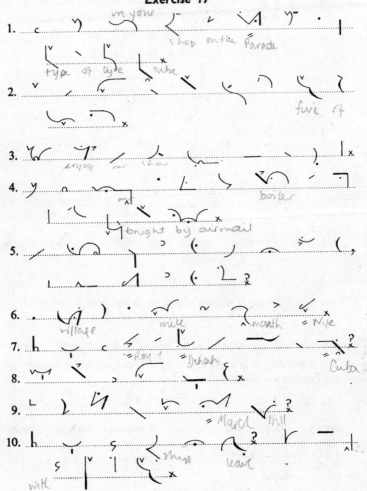

1.

2.

3.

4.

5.

6.

7.

8.

9.

10.

11.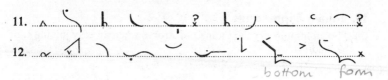

12.

bottom form

Exercise 18

1. What do you think we ought to do? I think we should give them a month in which to pay the bill

2. If you wish to catch the boat you will have to leave early

3. I think you will have to buy a coil for your car.

4. If you can arrive at five you will be in time for the talk

5. I have no wish to annoy you but I think the debt should be paid

6. I admire the type of youth who will do a job thoroughly.

7. For a low outlay, you can get a couch for the room.

8. A cure for the lazy boy would be to get him a job which would keep him busy.

9. Why have you allowed your bill to go unpaid?

10. What can we do for you?

11. You can read and write for an hour.

12. How can we keep in touch with them when they go away

13. Why do you think it would be the wrong thing to do?

14. I think you are right, and you may have to show why you are making the change

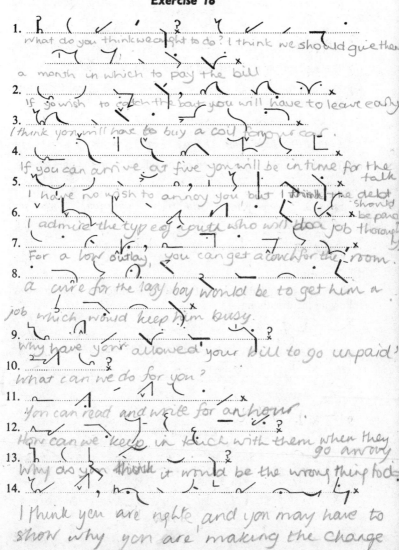

18. Joined Diphthongs

(a) The diphthong signs are joined to strokes when an easy joining can be made—

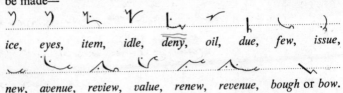

ice, eyes, item, idle, deny, oil, due, few, issue,

new, avenue, review, value, renew, revenue, bough or bow.

(b) The sign for *ow* is contracted in the word ⌣ *now.*

(c) The sign for *i* is contracted before *l, m, k,* and upward *r* to form such phrases as—

VOWEL RETAINED

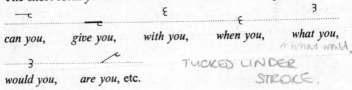

I will (I'll), I am (I'm), I may, I can, I write.

(d) The short form *you* is turned on its side to form the phrases—

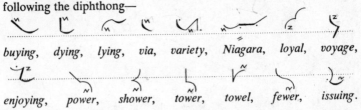

can you, give you, with you, when you, what you,

would you, are you, etc.

TUCKED UNDER STROKE.

19. Triphones

A small tick added to a diphthong sign indicates another vowel following the diphthong—

buying, dying, lying, via, variety, Niagara, loyal, voyage,

enjoying, power, shower, tower, towel, fewer, issuing.

Exercise 19

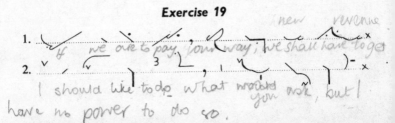

1.

2.

I should like to do what would ask, but I have no power to do so.

It will be your duty to check each item we charge

3.

4.

I shall go to the automobile show and I may buy a new car

5.

Do you wish to renew your fire policy? It would be due

6.

I am awarded the value of a shop window and the avenue

7.

I will give you a cheap rate to Niagara via the Lake route

8.

What would be your rate for a large room with bathe shower

9.

We had a fire and our factory was idle for a month so we had a poor year

10.

I have no wish to argue with you; you may be right

11.

You will rub your eyes when you see our New Eurocar in what you say

Distinctive Outlines: ___ *pure,* ___ *poor.*

NB.

12.

Why are you buying a poor type of oil when you can get a pure oil for your money.

13.

Poor oil may damage your car; it will pay you to buy a purer variety.

Exercise 20

Would you like to go to America with me in July

I know you will thoroughly enjoy the tour if you can come with me

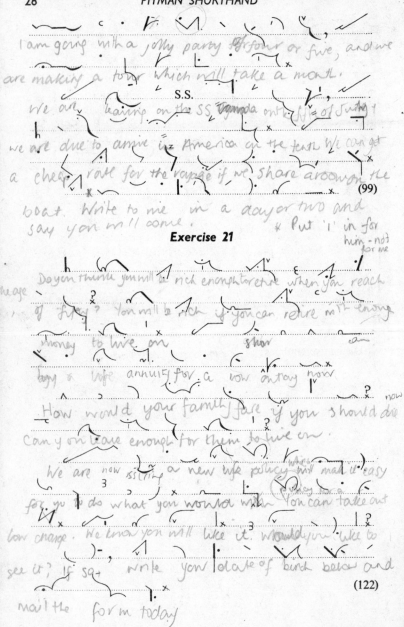

I am going with a jolly party of four or five, and we are making a tour which will take a month.

We are leaving on the S.S. Vampa on the 9th of June; we are due to arrive in America on the tenth. We can get a cheaper rate for the voyage if we share a room in the boat. Write to me in a day or two and say you will come. (99)

Exercise 21

*Put 'I' in for him – not for me

Do you think you will be rich enough to retire when you reach the age of fifty? You will be rich if you can retire with enough money to live on, or buy a life annuity for a sum that you have now. How would your family fare if you should die now? Can you leave enough for them to live on.

We are now issuing a new life policy which has made it easy for you to do what you would with. You can take out a policy which you can change. We know you will like it. Would you like to see it? If so, write your date of birth below and mail the form today (122)

20. Consonant H

Letter	Sign	Name	As in
H	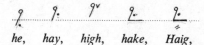	hay	he, high, hay
		hay	hope, happy, head

(a) When *h* is the only consonant stroke, or is followed by *k* or *g*, use the downward form—

he,   *hay,*   *high,*   *hake,*   *Haig,*

and also in the derivatives of words written with the downward *h*—

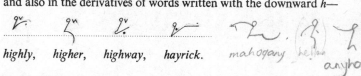

highly,   *higher,*   *highway,*   *hayrick.*   *mahogany*   *hellhole*   *anyhow*

(b) Use the upward form when *h* is joined to other consonants—

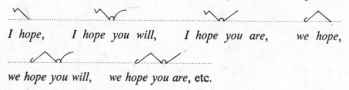

happy,   *hope,*   *head,*   *heavy,*   *hotel,*   *hang,*   *huge,*   *hurry.*

(c) The word *hope* is contracted to the stroke *p* to form the phrases

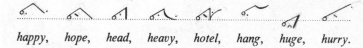

I hope,   *I hope you will,*   *I hope you are,*   *we hope,*

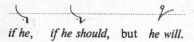

we hope you will,   *we hope you are,* etc.

(d) The word *he* is represented in the middle or at the end of a phrase by the short form ___ In other cases ___ is used.

if he,   *if he should,*   but   *he will.*

Exercise 22

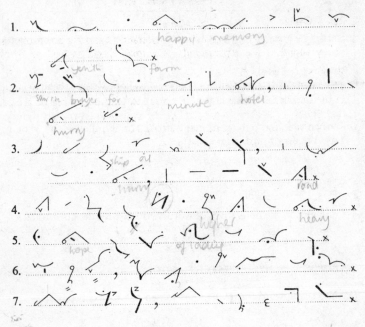

1. happy memory

2. youth farm / saw th buyer for / minute hotel / hurry

3. ships oil / hurry / road

4. higher / heavy

5. hope / of totally

6.

7.

Exercise 23

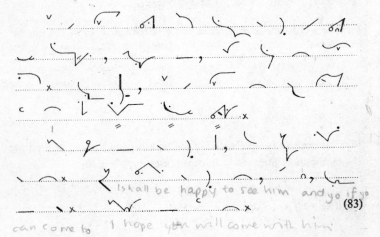

I shall be happy to see him and yo if yo (83)
can come to   I hope you will come with him

CHAPTER VIII

21. S Circle

The very frequently occurring consonant *s*, and its corresponding heavy sound *z*, are represented by a small circle as well as by the strokes ⟩ and ⟩

The small circle joins easily to other consonant strokes at the beginning, in the middle, or at the end of a word. At the beginning of a word, the *s* circle is always read first; at the end of a word, the *s* circle is always read last.

The *s* circle is written inside a curve—

(a) face, these, shoes, loss, knows, names, bills,

else, anxious, less, months, leaves, shows, lose,

miss, arms, ears, nice, size, voice, invoice,

announce, advice, news, views, refuse, items,

issues, errors, forms, office, affairs.

(b) safe, seem, slow, song, silk, sir, small,

Sunday, sense, sale, sales, save, saving, sell,

selling, sleep, snow, some, soon, sun, since,

similar, soil, south, sign, salary.

(c) message, absence, business, cousin, reason, receive,

31

receiving, passing, dozen, inside, music, Wednesday.

SHORT FORMS

has or as, his or is, several, those, this, thus.

NOTE: has the or as the, is the.

Exercise 24

1. *your message, invoices, of lading ready, ship sails = Wednesday*

2. *Since the business for the year shows a heavy loss, the bank may wish to have a voice in the firm's affairs*

3. *refuse to pay this sum, when we can get the same items for less.*

4. *may we know why this small bill is still unpaid. As you know we have allowed it to go beyond the usual time, happy to give you details of any of the items which appear on the bill.*

5. *hope to add the names of a dozen firms which will sell our silk.*

6. *I have seen the head of the firm, & I think he will renew the lease on the office in South Avenue.*

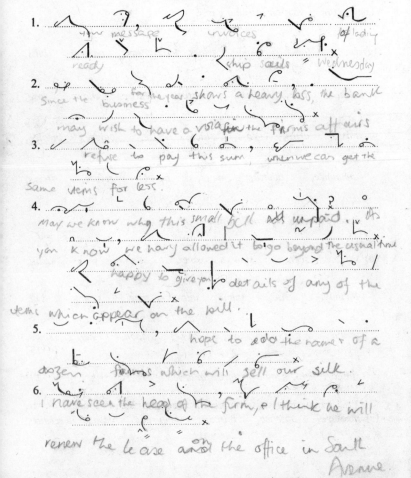

7. *(shorthand outlines)*
He will, I think, wish to learn few rooms and those effect a saving

8. *(shorthand outlines)*
It is firm has had a poor year and for this reason he has to save some money

9. *(shorthand outlines)*
happy give you names of those hotels which have bought them

Exercise 25

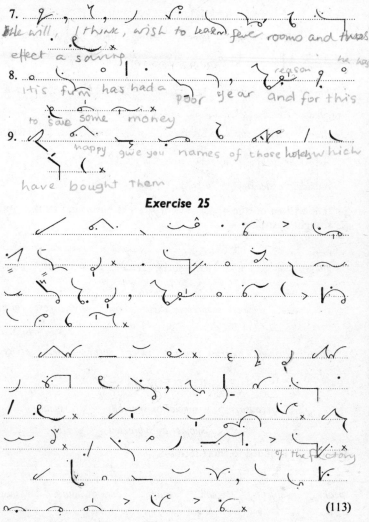

(113)

22. The *s* circle is written with a left (anti-clockwise) motion to straight strokes.

(*a*) This means that it is written on the right side of straight down-strokes—

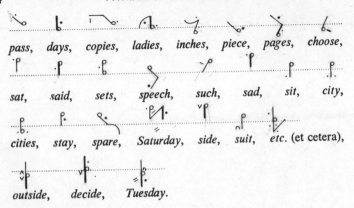

pass, days, copies, ladies, inches, piece, pages, choose,

sat, said, sets, speech, such, sad, sit, city,

cities, stay, spare, Saturday, side, suit, *etc.* (et cetera),

outside, decide, Tuesday.

(b) It is written on the upper side of straight horizontal strokes and straight upstrokes—

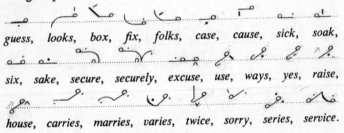

guess, looks, box, fix, folks, case, cause, sick, soak,

six, sake, secure, securely, excuse, use, ways, yes, raise,

house, carries, marries, varies, twice, sorry, series, service.

SHORT FORMS

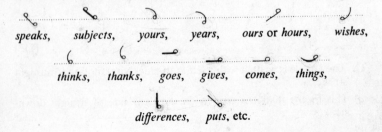

because,   special or specially,   speak,

subject or subjected.

The *s* circle is added to short forms—

speaks,   subjects,   yours,   years,   ours or hours,   wishes,

thinks,   thanks,   goes,   gives,   comes,   things,

differences,   puts, etc.

Exercise 26

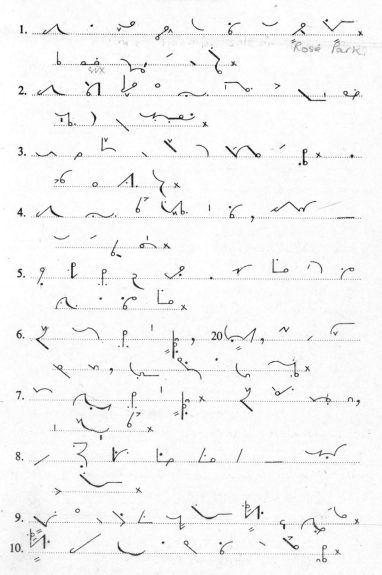

Exercise 27

1. my book, "which will be ready soon gives my news on the subject The "Music of our Times"

2. I hope to give a series of talks on several different cities and I have chosen this subject for my talks.

3. If I write out the names of the cities and the dates on which I am to speak, can you type the schedule for me? I should like to have two copies.

4. I shall be happy if you will type a copy of my speech for me. It is forty pages in length.

5. How long does it take to type such a long speech? Can you have it ready for me in two hours?

6. The head of the firm said "I am going to give you a higher salary because of the absence of errors in the jobs I have given you to do."

7. Thank you for your news. Many thanks too for the magazine. I am happy to know you are having a nice time.

8. I enjoy reading two special items in the magazine.

"The Way Things Seem To Me" and "News Outside the Door."

9. *We owe several large items on this months bills which ought to be paid in a few days*

10. *May we know soon what you decide to do? What would be the worthing to do!*

23. Final *s* circle represents the word *us* in such phrases as—

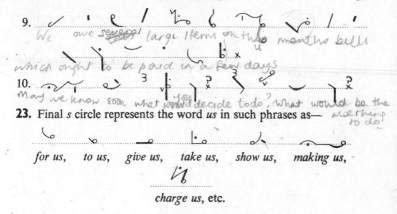

for us, to us, give us, take us, show us, making us,

charge us, etc.

NOTE: with us, when is, when is the, what is, what is the.

Exercise 28

1. *We rise to be of service to you, and we shall be happy to change the shoes if you will mail them*

2. *May we know when you will have the new designs for the ladies suits ready for us?*

3. *What is because of the delay? You seem to be slow in making them up?*

4. *You will receive them in a few days. We hope you will excuse the delay.*

5. *We are slow because of our desire to give you designs which will be different new, and it takes many hours to make them.*

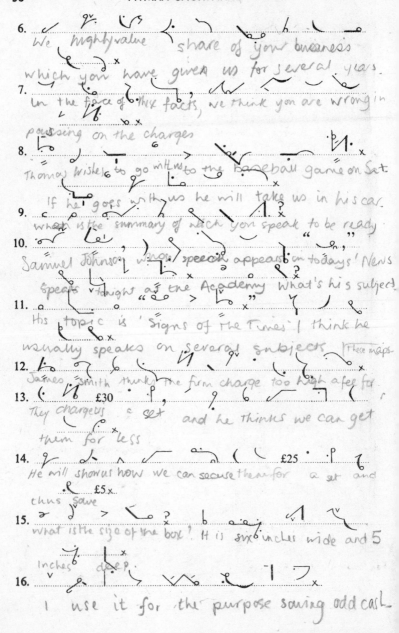

6. We highly value share of your business which you have given us for several years.

7. In the face of these facts, we think you are wrong in passing on the charges

8. Thomas wishes to go with us to the baseball game on Sat. If he goes with us he will take us in his car.

9. When is the summary of which you speak to be ready

10. Samuel Johnson, whose speech appears in todays' News speaks tonight at the Academy What's his subject

11. His topic is "Signs of the Times" I think he usually speaks on several subjects. These maps

12. James Smith thinks the firm charge too high a fee for

13. They charge us £30 a set and he thinks we can get them for less

14. He will show us how we can secure them for a set and £25 thus save £5.

15. What is the size of the box? It is six inches wide and 5 inches deep.

16. I use it for the purpose saving odd cash

24. The *s* circle is written on the outside of the angle formed by two straight strokes—

desk,   discuss,   dispose,   besides,   opposite,   justice,

sixty,   succeed,   receipt,   history.

25. The circle at the beginning of a word represents *s* only.

In the few words beginning with *z*, the stroke *z* is used—

zeal,   zero,   zenith, etc.

Exercise 29

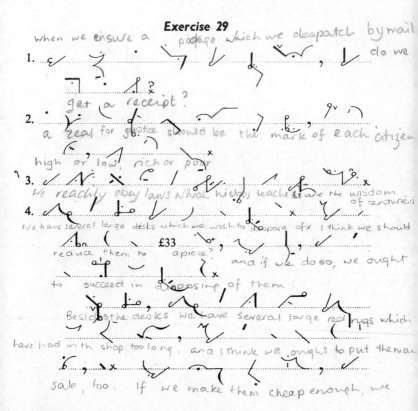

1. when we ensure a package which we despatch by mail, do we get a receipt?

2. a zeal for justice should be the mark of each citizen, high or low, rich or poor

3. We readily obey laws which history teaches us are the wisdom of centuries

4. We have several large desks which we wish to dispose of. I think we should reduce them to £33 apiece, and if we do so, we ought to succeed in disposing of them

Besides the desks we have several large red rugs which have had in th shop too long, and I think we ought to put them on sale, too. If we make them cheap enough, we

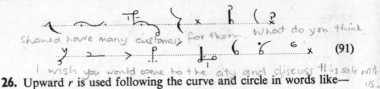

Should have many customers for them. What do you think

(91)

I wish you would come to the city and discuss this sale with us.

26. Upward *r* is used following the curve and circle in words like—

officer,   answer,   sincere,

even though the words do not end with a vowel; because a much more swiftly written and readable outline is obtained in this way. (See p. 18.)

27. The stroke *l* may easily be written downward, and when it precedes or follows circle *s* attached to a curve it is written in the same direction as the circle—

vessel, nicely, cancel, council, lesson, noiseless, muscle, loosely.

Exercise 30

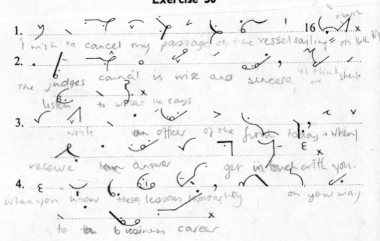

1. *I wish to cancel my passage on the vessel sailing on 16th*

2. *The judges council is wise and sincere, I think sharp listen to what he says*

3. *write an officer of the firm today + When I receive your answer get in touch with you.*

4. *When you know these lessons thoroughly on your way to the business career*

CHAPTER IX

28. St Loop

(a) A small loop, written in the same direction as the *s* circle, represents *st* (called "stee")—

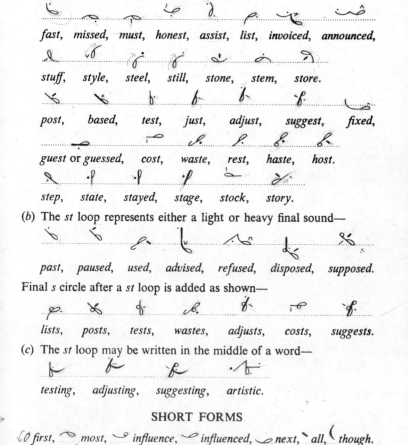

fast, missed, must, honest, assist, list, invoiced, announced,

stuff, style, steel, still, stone, stem, store.

post, based, test, just, adjust, suggest, fixed,

guest or *guessed, cost, waste, rest, haste, host.*

step, state, stayed, stage, stock, story.

(b) The *st* loop represents either a light or heavy final sound—

past, paused, used, advised, refused, disposed, supposed.

Final *s* circle after a *st* loop is added as shown—

lists, posts, tests, wastes, adjusts, costs, suggests.

(c) The *st* loop may be written in the middle of a word—

testing, adjusting, suggesting, artistic.

SHORT FORMS

first, most, influence, influenced, next, all, though.

NOTE: *although, all right, already, always, almost, also, as fast as.* at first a first of all

in the first place. cost caused

Exercise 31

Distinctive Outlines:  cost, caused.

1. *assist* ... *itemised list* ... *all the*

stock

2. *The bill last hand* ... *store* *store the of each item*

3. ... *refused* *lessa*

service

4. *Honest value* ... *secure* *buyers*

5. *subjected*

6. *step* ... *waste as fast as* *suggest adjusting* ... *next step*

7.

8. *unnoticed* *steel posts* ... *stone posts*

9. *caused* ... *schedule* *cancel*

10. *confluence*

11. *In the past we have* ... *style* *pencil*

12.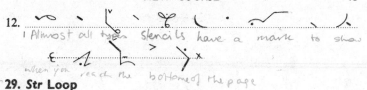

I Almost all types Stencils have a mark to show when you reach the bottom of the page

29. Str Loop

A large final loop, written in the same direction as the *s* circle, represents *ster—* USUALLY FINAL, SOMETIMES MIDDLE NEVER START

3/4 stroke

master, register, faster, poster, minister, administer,

investor, Leicester, Chester, Rochester, coaster, roadster.

The *ster* loop is not used at the beginning of a word.

The *s* circle is added for such words as—

masters, registers, posters, investors.

Exercise 32

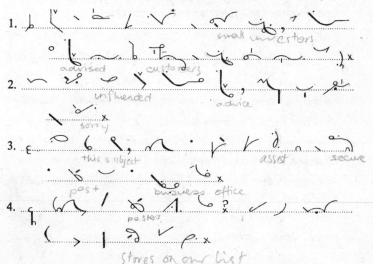

1. *small investors — advised customers*

2. *unfluenced advice — sorry*

3. *this s ubject — assist — secure — post — business office*

4. *posters — Stores on our list*

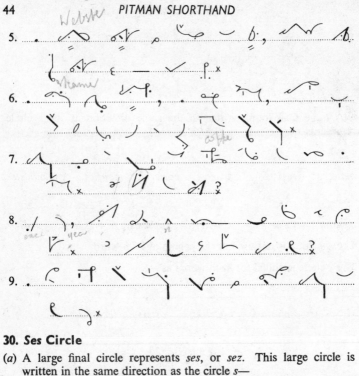

30. Ses Circle

(a) A large final circle represents *ses*, or *sez*. This large circle is written in the same direction as the circle *s*—

faces, losses, services, cases, pieces, boxes, taxes, success, passes, fixes, causes, uses, chooses, supposes.

(b) The large circle also represents *ses* in the middle of a word—

necessary, necessity, successive, successfully.

(c) Any vowel other than short *ĕ* between the two *s*'s is indicated by writing the vowel sign inside the circle—

basis, insist, exhaust, resist, census, exercise, exercises.

SHORT FORMS

themselves, *ourselves*, *as is*, *is as*, *myself*,

himself, *itself*, *much.*

yourself

Exercise 33

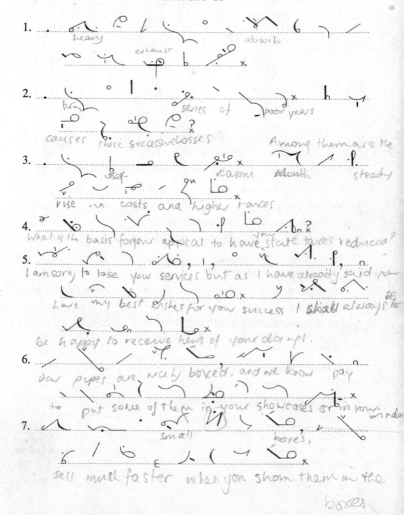

1. heavy ... absorb ... exhaust

2. firm ... series of ... poor years ... causes these successive losses. Among them are the

3. ... reasons ... Month ... steady rise in costs and higher taxes.

4. What is the basis for your appeal to have your state taxes reduced?

5. I am sorry to lose your services but as I have already said, you have my best wishes for your success. I shall always be happy to receive news of your doings.

6. Our pipes are nicely boxed, and we know pay to put some of them in your showcases or in your window.

7. small ... boxes, sell much faster when you show them in the boxes.

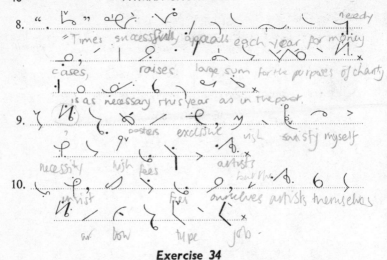

8. "*Times* successfully appeals each year for money
cases, raises large sum for the purposes of charity
is as necessary this year as in the past.

9. posters exclusive wish satisfy myself
necessity high fees artists

10. but the artist
artist even ourselves artists themselves
our how type job.

Exercise 34

(*Write in Shorthand*)

(*Phrases are indicated by hyphens. Short Forms are indicated by italic type.*)

1. *Are-you* enjoying *your* study *of-this subject*? *I-hope-you-are.*

2. *When you-can* write these exercises fast, *you-will-be on-your* way *to*-making *your* living *in a* business office.

3. Besides *its* value *to-you, I-hope-you* like-*the subject for-itself.*

4. *As you* know, *this subject is* widely used *in* business offices, *but it-has* many uses besides *this.*

5. *You-can* use *it for*-many *different* purposes. *Can-you* name some *of-them*?

6. *The* success *of*-many *a* famous head *of a large* business firm *is* due *to-his* study *of-this subject. It-was-the first* step *in-his* business career.

7. Write-*the* signs *as*-fast-*as you-can. A*lways read back *what you*-write.

8. Each time *you-*write *an* exercise *you-should* write *it* faster *and* read *it* back faster.

9. Write-*the* forms just-*as* they appear *in-this* book.

10. *In*-time *you-*may, if-*you wish*, write these same forms *as*-fast-*as you-can* speak.

31. Sw Circle

(*a*) A large initial circle represents *sw* (called "sway"). The *sw* circle is written in the same direction as the *s* circle—

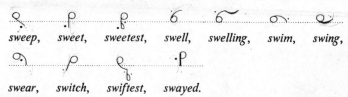

sweep,   sweet,   sweetest,   swell,   swelling,   swim,   swing,

swear,   switch,   swiftest,   swayed.

(*b*) The *sw* circle represents the words *as we* in such phrases as—

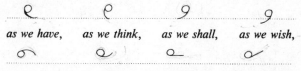

as we have,   as we think,   as we shall,   as we wish,

as we may,   as we know,   as we can,   as we are, etc.

It is also used to form the phrase 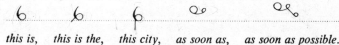 as well as.

(*c*) The large circle represents the two *s*'s in such phrases as—

this is,   this is the,   this city,   as soon as,   as soon as possible.

SHORT FORMS

_____ United States,   _____ New York,   _____ largest.

Special Phrase: _____ United States of America.

Exercise 35

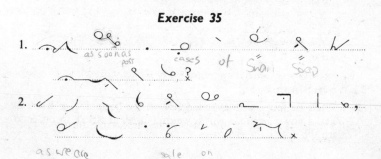

3. *This is* ... *as well now* ... *emphasise* ... *self readily*

4. *Swan is not supposed to sing a sweet song when it is dying. This is said to be the sweetest song it sings and this is the story which has given us the famous Swan Song.*

5. *N.Y. is the largest city in the United States. If you go to the top of any of the high towers of this city you will have a view which takes in all the city as well as the suburbs for many miles*

6. *monster ships which come to this city at the bay. They unload huge cargoes on the docks and take away with them similar loads when they leave.*

7. *In this city the business life of the = reaches its peak*

8. *As we are going to the docks, we can look at the new vessel. this is the swiftest as well as the largest of the steamers.*

9. *We may switch some of our business to the new firm as they will give us value as well as service*

10. *As we have seen, in the past, a steady pole usually sweeps many new officers in to the different staffs offices*

32. Vowel Indication

(*a*) A circle or loop is always read first at the beginning of a word. When a vowel begins a word, we must write a stroke in order to place the initial vowel sign—

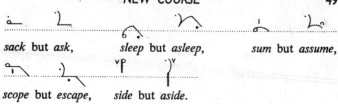

sack but *ask*,   sleep but *asleep*,   sum but *assume*,

scope but *escape*,   side but *aside*.

(b) A circle or loop is always read last at the end of a word. When a word ends in a vowel, we must write a stroke in order to place the final vowel sign—

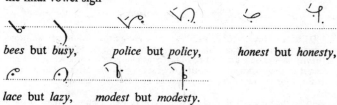

bees but *busy*,   police but *policy*,   honest but *honesty*,

lace but *lazy*,   modest but *modesty*.

(c) When a vowel occurs between *s* and *t*, the *st* loop is not used—

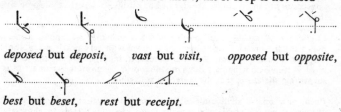

deposed but *deposit*,   vast but *visit*,   opposed but *opposite*,

best but *beset*,   rest but *receipt*.

The outline thus indicates the presence or absence of a vowel sound.

(d) As there are no places alongside a circle or loop for placing vowel signs, we must write—

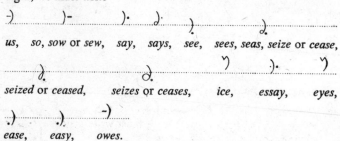

us,   so, *sow* or *sew*,   say,   says,   see,   sees, *seas*, *seize* or *cease*,

seized or *ceased*,   seizes or *ceases*,   ice,   essay,   eyes,

ease,   easy,   owes.

Special Phrases: *so much,* *too much,* *how much,* [Can't join these 3.]

as much as, *inasmuch as,* *as much as possible,*

[NB- such as when on line]

as early as possible, *as far as possible.*

SHORT FORMS

especial or *especially,* *language* or *owing,* *young,* [est stel]

anything, *nothing,* *something.*

NOTE: In Pitman Shorthand we represent all the consonants we hear in the words we write. Except for the "short forms," where for the sake of extreme brevity we use only one or two of the consonants in a word, we do not normally resort to the expedient of writing only some part of a word. This is one of the reasons for the remarkable legibility of Pitman Shorthand.

As we proceed we shall find that the various abbreviating devices of the system enable us to represent all the consonants in words in concise, legible, and rapid shorthand forms. These outlines are so clearly distinctive that it is unnecessary to insert the vowel signs. The outlines are perfectly legible without them.

In addition to writing a full outline of the consonants, we employ a means of indicating the presence or absence of a vowel with very nearly every abbreviating device of the system. Another expedient, highly prized by the fastest and most accurate shorthand writers in the world, is position writing. It is not surprising, therefore, that the system is so legible.

From now on we shall omit all but essential vowel signs in the shorthand exercises; but we shall take care to insert essential vowels to eliminate any possibility of hesitation in reading back shorthand notes.

Exercise 36

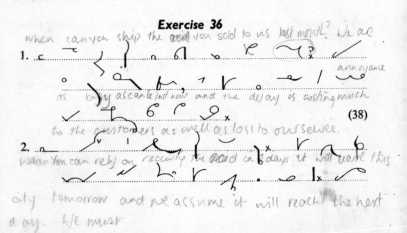

1. [when can you ship the ___ you sold to us last month? We are as busy as can be just now and the delay is costing much (annoyance) to the customers as well as loss to ourselves.] (38)

2. [When you can rely on receiving the ___ in 8 days it will leave this city tomorrow and we assume it will reach the next day. We must]

apologise for the delay. Owing to the heavy loss caused by the fire at our factory last month our stocks became too low. We are making up for lost time as fast as we can (63)

Exercise 37

as early as possible essences,

(60)

Exercise 38

(86)

Exercise 39

1. to do something to assist you Jackson Can you do anything to induce him to make a thorough study of the language? I know

you will be ready *to* assist *him* as much as poss *and I*
know he will be influenced by your advice   (47)

2.
In as much as it is necessary in this subject *to* deal extensively *with*
the language, he should see *that* how easy it is *to* study as far as poss
such things do style and *the* best-usage business houses *is* se
a high value on ability *to* use a language in *the* right way Because
so much emphasis *is* being given *to* ability, he should resolve
to make himself as far as poss a master *of the* best form. Now
his language sense is poor, but when he knows how much it may effect
his career, I know he will do all he can *to* remedy   (115)
as soon as possible *the* errors he makes.

Exercise 40

(Write in Shorthand)

1. Suppose some big customer *of-yours* ceased *to-deal-with-you.*
What-would you do? We-think-you would write *to-him,* asking if-*he*
had *any special* reason *for-his* silence.

2. *This-is* what *we-are-*now asking-*you. Although in-the* past *our*
business *with-you in-this-*city *was* extensive, *several* months *have*
elapsed since *you* last *had any* dealings *with-us. We* should like *to*
know *why, as-we-are* unaware *of any* failure *to-give-you-the* best
service.

3. *We al*ways desire *to-*satisfy *all-our* customers, *large* buyers
or small. *We* assure-*you we-shall-do anything we-can* to put *things*
right, if-*you think our* service *in-any-*way faulty.   (118)

Exercise 41

(*Write in Shorthand*)

1. *I-have-*seen *your* notice *in to-*day's "Star," *and-I should-*like *to-have* details *of-your* new Masters' Reading Series. *I-think* such *a* series *should* make *a* wide appeal, *and-I-wish-you much* success *with-it.*

2. Many *of-those* who *have-*seen my set *of* "Stories *of-the* Earth, Sea, *and* Sky" *speak* highly *of-it, and-several, I-*know, *have* bought similar sets *for-themselves.*

3. *I-*am-sorry *you have* allowed "Poster Designing" *to-*go out *of* stock. Such *a* book, *it-*seems *to-me, should-have a large* sale, *as* so-many *are-*now taking-up-*the* study *of-this-subject. In-*view *of-this,* may *I* suggest *a* new issue?   (116)

CHAPTER X

33. Halving *- shape stays - half size*

Strokes are halved to indicate a following *t* or *d*.

(a) In words of one *syllable* a light stroke is generally halved to indicate a following *t* but not a following *d*— *only preceding stroke is halved.*

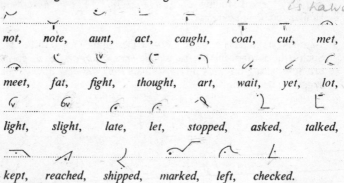

not, note, aunt, act, caught, coat, cut, met,

meet, fat, fight, thought, art, wait, yet, lot,

light, slight, late, let, stopped, asked, talked,

kept, reached, shipped, marked, left, checked.

NOTE: ⌣ *night.*

The *s* circle is always read last: ⌣ notes, ⌣ acts, ⌣ thoughts, ⌣ lots, ⌣ waits, ⌣ nights.

(b) In words of one *syllable* a heavy stroke is generally halved to indicate a following *d* but not a following *t*—

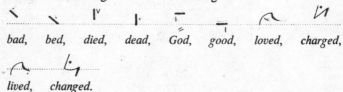

bad, bed, died, dead, God, good, loved, charged,

lived, changed.

SHORT FORMS

— quite, — could, ⟨ that, ⟨ without, ⟲ sent, ⟩ wished.

54

Exercise 42

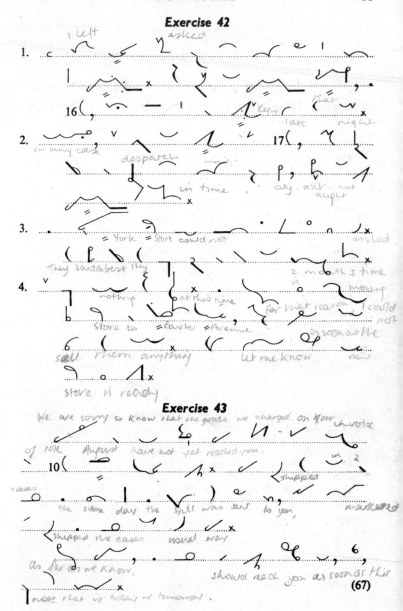

Handwritten shorthand outlines with interlinear longhand annotations:

1. i left — asked — e 1
   16(— replied — that — late night

2. in any case — despatch — mag — in time — 17(— city ask not night

3. =York =Store could not — visited — They said the best they — 2 months time is moving

4. nothing — at this time — for that reason I could not — Store to =Baxter =Avenue — 6 — sell them anything — let me know — as soon as the new store is ready

Exercise 43

We are sorry to know that the goods we charged on your invoice of 10th August have not yet reached you.
10(— shipped 2 cases — the same day the bill was sent to you, — marked — shipped the cases — usual way — as far as we know, — should reach you as soon as this — note that is today or tomorrow.

(67)

34. (*a*) In words of two or more syllables, a stroke is generally halved to indicate a following *t* or *d*—

(1) *attached, answered, except, suggested, avoid, market,*

recent, absent, admit, arrived, engaged, enjoyed,

estate, stated, exact, result, benefit, booklet.

(2) *actually, writing, badly, lately, entire, entirely,*

evidence, sometimes, waiting, certain, goodbye, absolutely.

(3) *omit, omitted, note, noted, accept, accepted, submit,*

submitted, await, awaited, limit, limited, visit,

visited, list, listed, remit, remitted, deduct, deducted,

notify, notified, invited.

(*b*) A half-length stroke is not written through the line to indicate a third position. Words like the following are written on the line—

east, feet, fit, sheets, bid, did, written, invite, indeed,

needed, instead, little, moved.

(c) Where a final diphthong is joined, a single stroke is generally halved to indicate a final *t* or *d*—

doubt, about, bowed, cute, issued.

Exercise 44

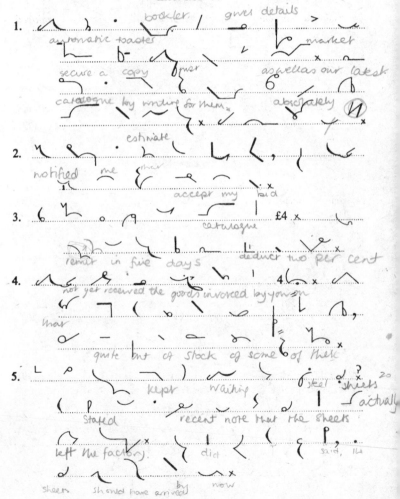

1. booklet. / gives details
automatic toaster / market
secure a copy your as well as our latest
catalogue by writing for them. absolutely

2. estimate
notified me that
accept my bid

3. catalogue £4
remit in five days deduct two per cent

4. not yet received the goods invoiced by you on
that
quite out of stock of some of these

5. kept waiting steel sheets actually
stated recent note that the sheets
left the factory. did said, the
sheets should have arrived by now

Exercise 45

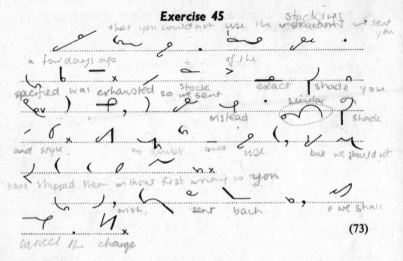

that you could not use the stockings we sent you a few days ago ... of the specified was exhausted so we sent stock ... exact shade you instead similar shade and style ... no doubt could use ... but we should not have shipped them without first writing to you ... wish, sent back ... we shall cancel the charge (73)

Exercise 46

having a benefit show next night. I am writing to invite you to come ... is badly needed for some special cases we have on our list and all the money is to be used for that purpose. The cost of the tickets is £1.50 each. I know that you will wish to assist the cause as much as possible that you will let me have your cheque for several tickets. (79)

Exercise 47

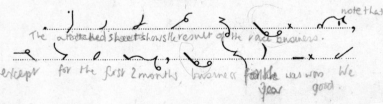

note that The attached sheet shows the result of the race answers. except for the first 2 months, business was good. We year

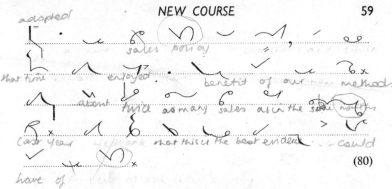

(80)

Exercise 48

(Write in Shorthand)

We-have-sent several notes *to-you* asking-*you* to pay-*the* bill *for-the*-goods *you* bought six-months-ago, *but-you* have-not answered *any of-them.*

We-are-sorry *to* say *that* now *we-shall-have* to-take-*the usual* steps *to*-avoid-*the* loss *of-our* money, if-*your* cheque is-not received by-*the first of next* month. *We* urge *you* to-mail *your* cheque *to-us without-*delay.

(74)

35. (*a*) To avoid confusion with ⟋ *should* and ⟋ *and*, we do not use ⟋ *rt* and ⟋ *rts* standing alone. Therefore we write—

rate,　rates,　right,　rights,　write,　wrote,　route.

(*b*) In certain words, where the proper length of a halved stroke would not clearly show, the halving principle is not employed—

fact,　effect,　liked,　locate,　minute,　select,　territory,　tonight.

(*c*) When a final vowel follows *t* or *d*, it is necessary to write the stroke *t* or *d* in order to place the vowel sign—

pity,　body,　forty,　window,　empty,　into,　Toronto.

Exercise 49

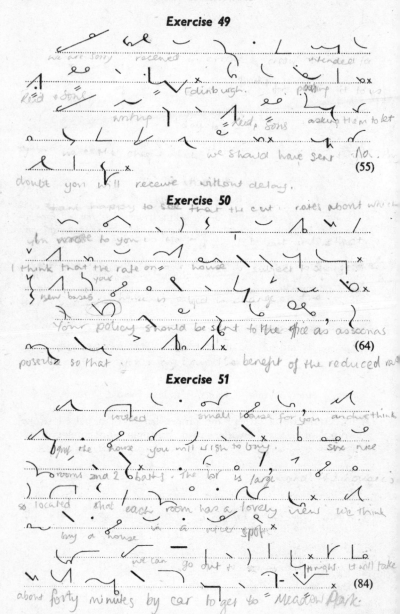

we are sorry   received   intended for

Reid & Sons   Edinburgh.   passing it to us

writing   Reid & Sons   asking them to let

we should have sent   No.
(55)

doubt you will receive without delay.

Exercise 50

I am happy to see that the cut rates about which

you wrote to you

I think that the rate on house

your

new bases.

Your policy should be sent to the office as soon as
(64)

possible so that you benefit of the reduced rate

Exercise 51

looked   small house for you and we think

buy the house you will wish to buy.   six nice

rooms and 2 baths. The lot is large

so located that each room has a lovely view we think

buy a house   nicer spot

we can go out   tonight. It will take
(84)

about forty minutes by car to get to Meadow Park.

Exercise 52

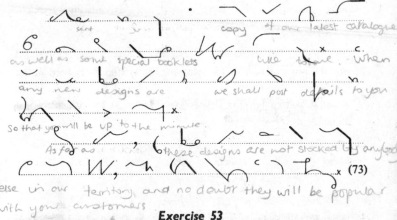

sent ... copy of our latest catalogue
6 as well as some special booklets ... like those. When
any new designs are ... we shall post details to you
So that you will be up to the minute.
As far as ... know these designs are not stocked by anybody (73)
else in our territory, and no doubt they will be popular
with your customers

Exercise 53

(Write in Shorthand)

Do-you know *that-we* sell good tyres? *It-is*-not-necessary *for-you* to buy tyres *in a* repair shop, *for our* store now carries *them*. *You-can* buy *them* when *you-are in-the* store, just-*as you* would select silks, or *something for-your* house.

These tyres *are* good value, *and*-they sell rapidly. Each *of-them* carries *our* guarantee. (63)

Exercise 54

(Write in Shorthand)

It-is quite some time since *you* bought *anything in-this* store. *I-am*-writing *to-you* myself, *because I should-be* sorry *to*-lose *your* custom.

It-may-be *that-we-have* offended *you in*-some-way. *If-this-is-the* case, *I*-hope-*you*-will write *to-me*. *Our* service *and our* way *of-do*ing business *are things which-we* boast about. *It-would-be* a pity *to* stay away *because of-something* which *could-be* easily remedied, *and you-should*-not hesitate *to*-write *to-me and* let-*me*-know-*the* cause. (95)

36. Downward L

Usually *l* is written upward.

(1) For convenience, *l* is usually written downward after *n* or *ng*—

only,   unless,   until,   canal,   analysis,   exceedingly,   annual,

evidently,   unfortunately,   recently,   certainly,   Nelson.

(2) For the purpose of vowel indication, *l* is written downward in the following two cases—

(*a*) When an initial vowel comes before *l*, and the *l* is followed by a simple horizontal stroke—

alone,   along,   Allen,   alike,   elm,   elect,   elected,

but *long,   like,   lake,   lime.*

(*b*) When *l* follows *f, v, sk,* or a straight upstroke, and a vowel does not end the word—

fail,   fall,   awful,   feel,   feeling,   fell,   fill,   full,   veal,

skill,   rule,   scale,   barrel,   successful,   useful,   rail.

When a vowel ends the word, *l* is written upward—

folly,   awfully,   fellow,   fully,   lovely,   successfully,

usefully,   yellow,   rely,   sickly.

Special Outlines: *volume,*   *column,*   *film.*

SHORT FORMS

inform-ed,   *never, November,*   *satisfactory,*

respect-ed,   *expect-ed,*   *inspect-ed-ion,*   *January,*

February,   *together,*   *altogether,*   *insurance.*

Exercise 55

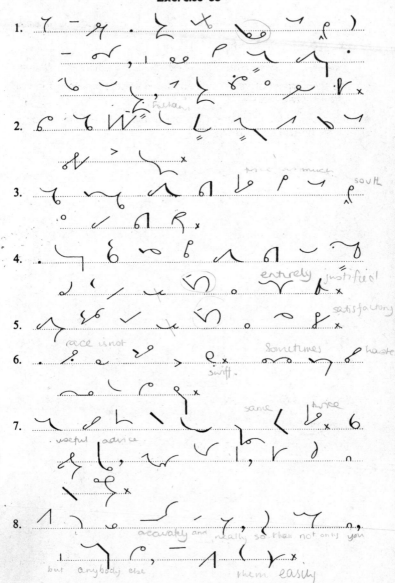

Exercise 56

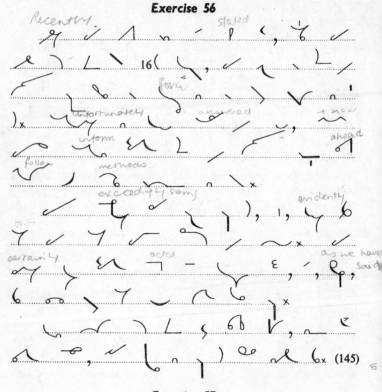

(145)

Exercise 57

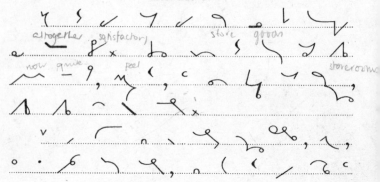

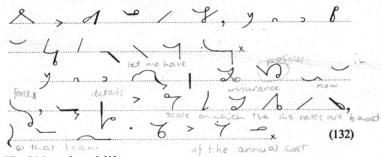

let me have

policies   in

force   details   insurance   now

scale on which the ins rates are based

so that I can.   of the annual cost   (132)

37. Abbreviated W

A small initial semicircle, written as shown, is used as an abbreviation for *w* at the beginning of *k*, *g*, *m*, and upward and downward *r*—

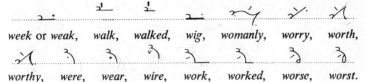

week or weak,   walk,   walked,   wig,   womanly,   worry,   worth,

worthy,   were,   wear,   wire,   work,   worked,   worse,   worst.

NOTE: The small semicircle is always read first. When a vowel begins a word, the stroke *w* must be written—

awake,   awoke,   aware.

Special Phrases: you were,   which were,   who were,

they were,   we were.

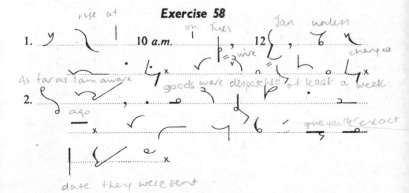

rise at

1.   10 a.m.   on Tues   Jan   unless

12   changed

As far as I am aware   goods were despatched at least a week

2.   ago   give you the exact

date they were sent

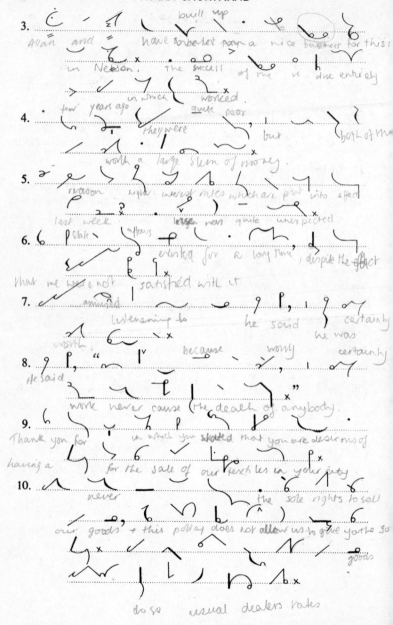

3. _Allan_ and _=_ have to market pay a nice business for this built up. in Nelson. The success of the is due entirely in which worked. few years ago quite poor

4. they were, but both of the worth a large sum of money.

5. reason higher interest rates which are put into effect last week was not quite unexpected.

6. state affairs existed for a long time, despite the effect that we were not satisfied with it

7. amused listening to he said certainly worth, because he was

8. He said "" because worry certainly work never cause (the death of anybody).

9. Thank you for in which you stated that you are desirous of having a for the sale of our textiles in your city.

10. never the sole rights to sell our goods + this policy does not allow us to give you the so goods do so usual dealers rates

Exercise 59

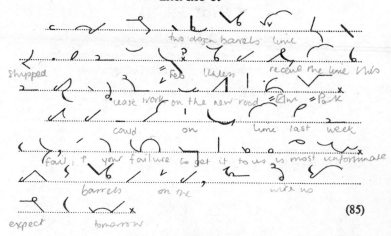

(85)

Exercise 60

(Write in Shorthand)

I-wish to-thank-you for-the catalogue *which-you-*were good-enough *to* post *to-me* recently. *Several* books listed *on* page 21 appear *to-be* just *what I-*am looking *for. I-have* marked *them on-the* attached sheet.

*Although I-think that-*these books *should-be* useful *to-me in-*my work, *I should* like *to inspect* them *to* see if-they *would-be satisfactory.* May *any of-the* books *be* sent back *to-you* if, *when I-have* looked at-*them, I-*decide *that-*they *would-*not-*be satisfactory for-*my purpose? (96)

CHAPTER XI

38. Double Consonants—*Pl Series*

A small beginning hook, written on the circle side of straight down-strokes and *k* and *g*, forms a series of double consonants—

These double consonants are called *pel*, *bel*, etc. The vowel signs are placed to them just as they are placed to single consonants—

play, place, places, placing, placed, replace,

plate, played, plus, blue, black, blame, blank,

block, class, clear, clerk, close, closed, enclose,

cloth, clothes, club, claim, glass, glad, single,

apply, applied, replied, simple, couple, able, enable,

double, table, reasonable, terrible, oblige, total,

entitled, include, included, including, local, uncle,

article, duplicate, o'clock.

Distinctive Outlines: valuable, available.

An *s* circle is written inside the hook of the *pl* series—

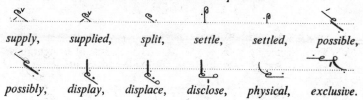

supply,   supplied,   split,   settle,   settled,   possible,

possibly,   display,   displace,   disclose,   physical,   exclusive.

SHORT FORMS

people,   belief, believe or believed,   tell,   till,   deliver, delivered or delivery,   call,   called,   equal or equally,   equalled or cold,   build or building (or able-to).

Phrases: at all,   by all,   I believe,   able to.

Exercise 61

1. simple advice saves you many hours of toil
   attached
   below post it
   local dealer details   (33)

2. Please supply samples of cloth blue + black,
   for autumn suits ifyou include
   a couple samples of single + double widths   (39)

3. deliver so entitled
   "Clothes + how to Make Them, supplied
   £75   (35)
   total cost including delivery.

4. [shorthand outline]

We are pleased [shorthand] be able to deliver some of the tables by the

ut of time [shorthand] supply rest in two

weeks [shorthand] obliged [shorthand] by the

[shorthand] (56)

enable us [shorthand] special [shorthand] display to them.

5. [shorthand outline]

I believe many articles in this sale should be

valuable to you. For the [shorthand] history of the

store, able to [shorthand] reasonably low

cost, [shorthand] I urge you call them as soon

you possibly can. Do not wait till it is too late. (61)

Exercise 62

1. called the house several times as much as each time I was unable [shorthand]

reply [shorthand] people were away

[shorthand] closed (30)

2. [shorthand]

replied [shorthand] Feb

goods supplied [shorthand] 12 [shorthand]

[shorthand] settled (35)

3. [shorthand]

cold storage

call and deliver them tell us to do so

reasonable. Let us store them

for you, worry about (46)

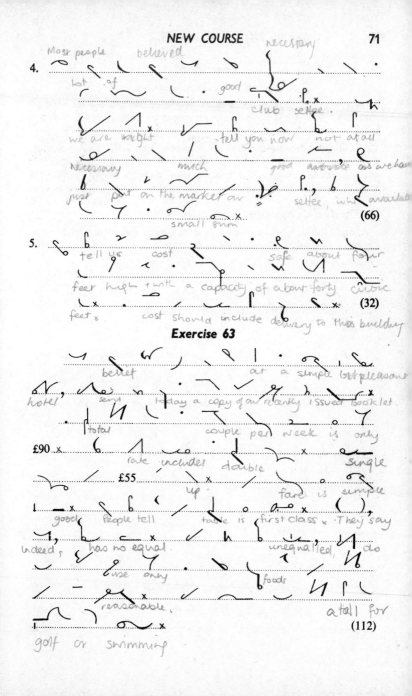

4. Most people believed necessary

lot of good club settee.

we are weight tell you now not at all

necessary much good attractive as we have

just put on the market our settee, which available

small sum (66)

5. tell us cost safe about four

feet high and with a capacity of about forty cubic

feet. cost should include delivery to this building (32)

Exercise 63

belief at a simple but pleasant

hotel, sent today a copy of our recently issued booklet.

total couple per week is only

£90. rate includes double single

£55 up. fare is simple

good. People tell table is first class. They say

indeed, has no equal unequalled, do

use only foods

reasonable. at all for

golf or swimming (112)

Exercise 64

(Write in Shorthand)

We-enclose *a* booklet *which gives* details *of-our* plate-glass window insurance. *When-you* renew *your* insurance *we-believe* *it*-will pay *you* *to*-take-out *this* type *of* policy.

You-will-note *that-we-are* able-to give-you *especially* useful service. *As*-soon-*as-we* receive *your* claim *we* replace-*the* glass. *Your* claim *is* settled *without*-delay, *and a* cheque *large* enough *to* pay *for all-the* damage, including *any* damage *to-your* window display, *is* sent *to-you*.

(83)

39. Double Consonants—*Pr Series*

A small initial hook, written on the non-circle side of straight down-strokes and *k* and *g*, forms a series of double consonants—

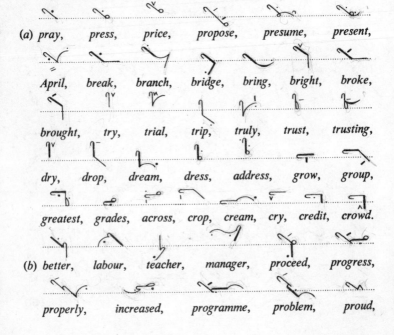

pr,   br,   tr,   dr,   chr,   jr,   kr,   gr.

These double consonants are called *per*, *ber*, etc.

(a) pray,   press,   price,   propose,   presume,   present,

April,   break,   branch,   bridge,   bring,   bright,   broke,

brought,   try,   trial,   trip,   truly,   trust,   trusting,

dry,   drop,   dream,   dress,   address,   grow,   group,

greatest,   grades,   across,   crop,   cream,   cry,   credit,   crowd.

(b) better,   labour,   teacher,   manager,   proceed,   progress,

properly,   increased,   programme,   problem,   proud, *degree,* *agreed,* *daughter,* *water,* *withdraw,*

practical, *liberal,* *graduate,* *October.*

SHORT FORMS

Dr., doctor, dear, during, truth, principal, principally or principle, liberty, member, remember or remembered, number or numbered, chair, cheer, care.

Exercise 65

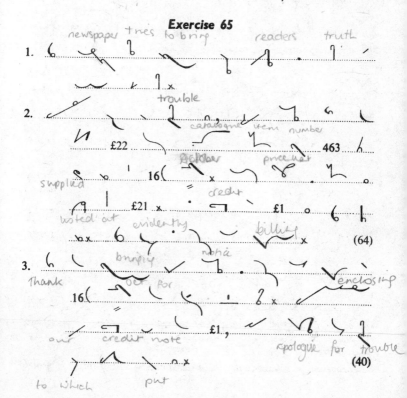

1. newspaper tries to bring readers truth

trouble

2. £22 catalogue item number 463
supplied 16 October price list
listed at £21 credit £1 evidently billing (64)

3. Thank bring notla 16 Oct for enclosing
our credit note £1, apologise for trouble
to which put (40)

4. [shorthand outlines]

member of our

Dear Sir, *we are glad*

club *manager*

liberty *you* *facilities until elected*

member. *is to be proposed next week*

(49)

truly

Exercise 66

April *propose* *increase the*

prices *number* *at present catalogue.*

increases *necessary 'cos* *high costs we* *now*

absorb *Your branch* *issue.*

catalogue *proceed with it until* *prices.*

Please remember that you must *list until* *post*

prices *issue*

(79)

Exercise 67

Dear Miss Black: *April* *brought out a*

series *history* *use*

forms 2. to 6 Those books solve many problems

teacher *treat* *bright* *practical way*

recall that *subject.*

series *better approach*

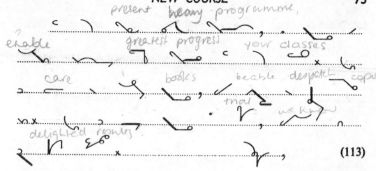

present heavy programme, enable greatest progress your classes care books beable despatch copies mal we know delighted results.

(113)

Exercise 68

(Write in Shorthand)

Dear Dr. Waters, *We-are* taking-*the liberty of* asking-*you to* address *our* graduates *on-*Monday, 29th-*January. Our principal and* teachers, *as-well-as-the* graduates, *would-be* proud *to-have-you deliver an* address. *We-*know-*that what-you-would tell-*us *as-the principal* speaker *on-our* programme *would-be remembered* by-*all our* graduates *for-*many-*years to-come.*

*We-*know-*that-you have* many *calls to-speak, and-that your* time *is* exceedingly valuable, *but-we-*feel *that-you-*will-be-glad *to-*talk *to-*us if-*you* possibly *can. We-*trust *that-you-*will-be-able-to accept. *Yours-*truly,   (107)

40. (a) When an initial circle or loop is written on the same side as the hook of the *pr* series, the *r* is included—

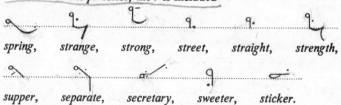

spring,   strange,   strong,   street,   straight,   strength,

supper,   separate,   secretary,   sweeter,   sticker.

(b) Both hook and circle are shown in the middle of a word—

extra,   extremely,   industry,   district,   express.

(c) When *skr* or *sgr* follows *t* or *d*, the combinations are written thus—

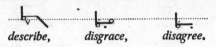

describe,   disgrace,   disagree.

Distinctive Outlines: *propriety*,   *property*,

propose,   *purpose*.

SHORT FORMS

description,   *surprise*,   *surprised*.

Exercise 69

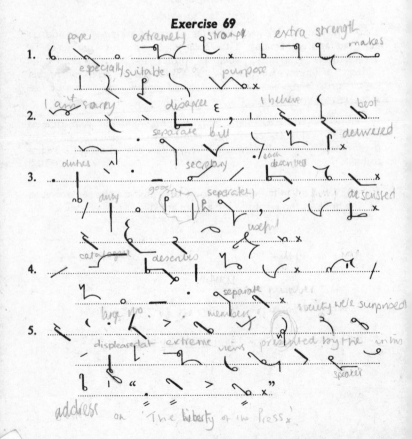

Exercise 70

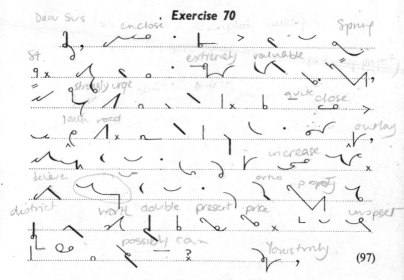

(97)

41. Special Use of Double Consonants

In a special group of words, the double consonant strokes are used although a distinct vowel comes between a consonant and hook *l* or hook *r*. The double consonant strokes are employed in order to secure briefer or more facile outlines. The most important of these words are given below.

Although it is seldom necessary to vocalize these special outlines, a dot vowel may be indicated by writing a small circle instead of the dot, either after or before the double consonant stroke—

parcel,   darling,   dark,   charm,   direct,   directly.

The short *ĕ* vowel is never indicated in words like ⟋ *person,* ⟋ *girl,* ⟋ *term.*

A dash vowel, or a diphthong, is shown by writing the vowel sign or diphthong sign through, or at the beginning or end of the stroke—

college,   accordance,   accordingly,   course,   court,   church, occurred, record, purchase, correct, collect, courtesy,

attorney, lecture, literature, lectures.

Distinctive Outlines: regard, regret.

Exercise 71

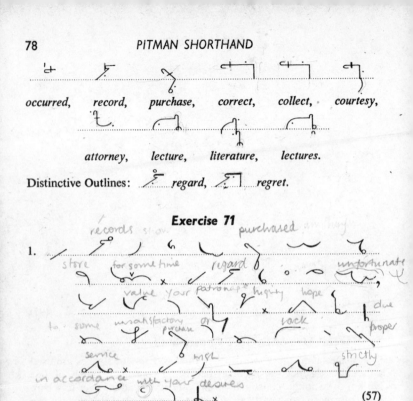

1. records show purchased any buy store for some time regard unfortunate value your patronage highly hope to some unsatisfactory purchase lack proper service with strictly in accordance with your desires

(57)

2. Several members club college faculty number necessary include extra course industry prospers because of the direct methods we employ with

3. customers tell them only truth describe products

4. steps to bring about passage buy retail labour problems I believe that can exercised by all not to obstruct this

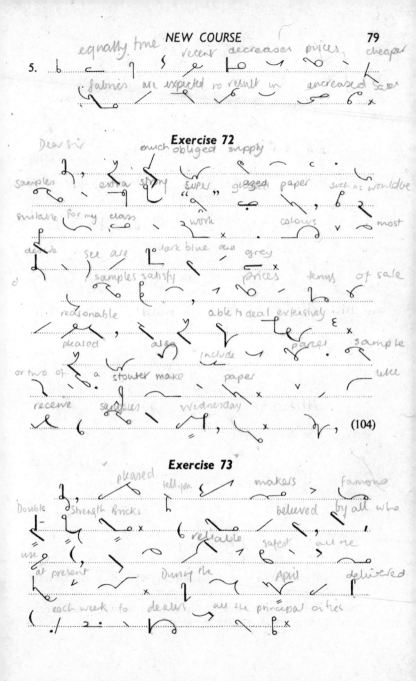

5. equally true recent decreases prices, cheaper fabrics are expected to result in increased sales.

Exercise 72

Dear sir much obliged supply samples extra strong "super" glazed paper such as would be suitable for my class work colours most desire see are dark blue and grey samples satisfy prices terms of sale reasonable able to deal extensively pleased also include parcel sample or two of a stouter make paper like receive samples Wednesday (104)

Exercise 73

pleased tell you makers famous Double Strength Bricks believed by all who use reliable safest all are at present During the April delivered each week to dealers all the principal cities

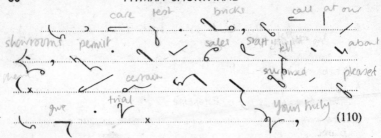

(110)

Exercise 74

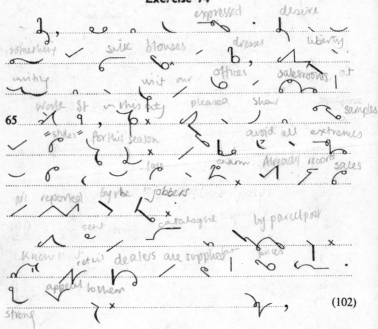

(102)

Exercise 75

(*Write in Shorthand*)

1. If-*you*-will bring *me a* supply *of*-samples *of-this* new breakfast food, *I*-will-try *to*-close-*the* deal *with-the* firm *myself*.

2. *During-the* course *of*-my lecture, *I-shall* try *to* show *how-the* progress of art *is* related *to-the* growth *of* industry.

3. *When I*-know *what-the* proposed water power scheme includes, *I-shall-be*-glad *to*-express my views.

4. *A* loud voice troubles *and* annoys us. Pleasant voices resemble sweet music.

5. Castles *in-the* air *are* fabrics *which* soon crumble, *but* dreamers *have* solved many *a* pressing problem.

6. Few *people are* able *themselves to* better-*the* labour *of-those* they blame.

Exercise 76
(*Write in Shorthand*)

Dear-Sirs, *Because-of-the* rapidly increasing cost *of* copper *and* steel, *we-are*-obliged *to* increase-*the* prices *of*-many *of-the* articles included *in our* catalogue. *We* extremely regret-*the* necessity *of* passing *on-the* higher charges *to-our* customers, *but* at-*the* present-time *this-is-the* only possible course *we-can* follow.

You-will-be notified *when* better terms *are* available *on-our* supplies, *and-we-are thus* enabled *to*-reduce-*the* prices. *Yours*-truly,   (79)

42. Double Consonants—*Curves*

(*a*) <u>A small initial hook, written on the inside of curves, forms a series of double consonant strokes</u>, *fr, vr*, etc.—

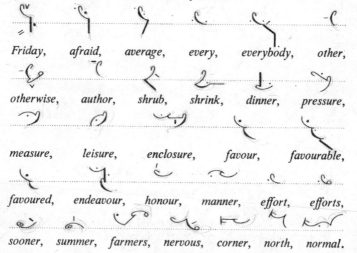

Friday,   afraid,   average,   every,   everybody,   other,

otherwise,   author,   shrub,   shrink,   dinner,   pressure,

measure,   leisure,   enclosure,   favour,   favourable,

favoured,   endeavour,   honour,   manner,   effort,   efforts,

sooner,   summer,   farmers,   nervous,   corner,   north,   normal.

(b) A large initial hook, written on the inside of curves, forms the double consonants *fl*, *vl*, etc.—

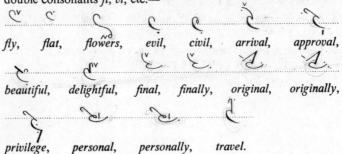

fly,   flat,   flowers,   evil,   civil,   arrival,   approval,

beautiful,   delightful,   final,   finally,   original,   originally,

privilege,   personal,   personally,   travel.

SHORT FORMS

nor (or in our),   near,   own,   owner,   more, remark or remarked,   remarkable,   Mr. or mere,   sure, pleasure,   larger,   largely,   everything,   over, however,   respectful-ly.

Exercise 77

This page contains shorthand (Pitman) outlines with English word cues written above them. The exercises are numbered 4, 5, 6 and Exercise 78 (items 1–5).

4. owe — favourabl — corner — suggest — over

5. near all transit facilities — you could not look — in our view — our store — more desirable spot

6. Manor Park — delightful place — spring — summer — full — trees — shrubs — flowers — No

Exercise 78

Please type — original — duplicate — list

1. Mr Skinner

2. expect — fly — Noal Bay — glad — meet — arrival — everything that is — about the case — to tell me — W

3. regret — unable deliver — goods — sooner — nor — Is it possible to say — at present can be — delivered

4. are you sure — enclosures were — envelope — Yes, I — personally

5. Either — shall have more space in some other building — or — over — entire floor in this building

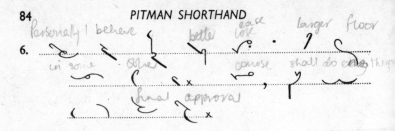

6.

Exercise 79

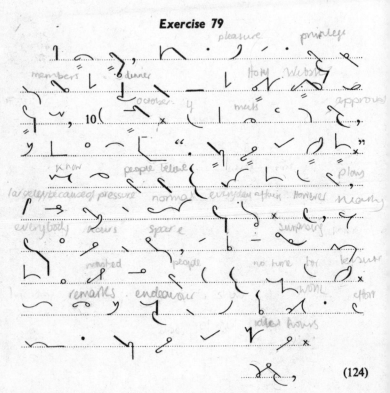

(124)

43. Additional Forms

(a) The double consonants *fr*, *vr*, *thr*, and *THr*, are represented by

) *fr*,) *vr*,) *thr*,) *THr* (reverse forms), as well as by

(*fr*, (*vr*, (*thr*, (*THr* (original forms).

VOWEL INDICATION RULE

When one of these double consonant strokes is the only stroke in the word, the reverse form is used *if the word does not begin with a vowel*—

free,   freight,   fruit,   three,   through,

INITIAL VOWELS:

but   *either,   ever,   offer,   offered,   other.*

(b) When joined to another stroke, the forms are used which join most conveniently. Usually, the reverse forms are joined to strokes written towards the right—

before,   bother,   leather,   brother,   cover,   covered,

discover,   forgot,   gather,   lever,   Hanover.

NOTE: *Thursday,   thirty,   fresh.*

(c) After *k, g, n,* or a straight upstroke, *fl* and *vl* are reversed—

rifle,   reflect,   naval,   novel,   rival,   cavalry.

44. The double consonant stroke *shl* is always written upward. The stroke *shr* is always written downward—

official,   shelf,   partial,   specialize,   speciality,   essential,

artificial,   pressure,   Fisher.

45. The heavy sign ⌣ is used to represent *ng-kr* or *ng-gr*—

thinker,   banker,   conquer,   finger,   stronger.

SHORT FORMS

from,   very,   they are,   their or *there.*

Exercise 80

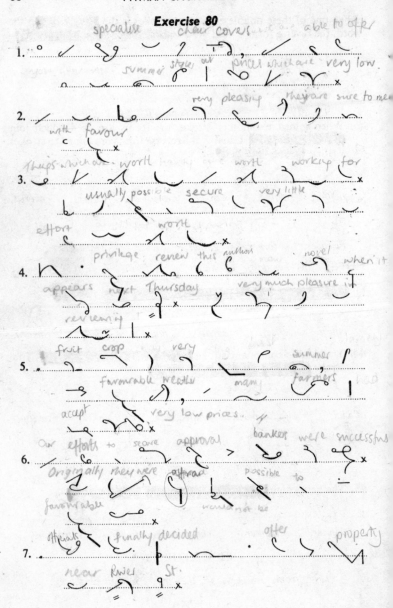

8. 'The special price at which goods are offered is as low as any ever reached. it scarcely covers the cost of freight before ;

9. circular prices enclosed that they are very reasonable.

There is a noticeable decrease in our business for the month of Feb.

10. Our Liverpool branch show drop almost = 30%

Exercise 81

1. From I gather bankers favour increasing the average rate to 3 % + in a unofficial manner endeavoured to influence others adopt this course.

2. author had travelled up the Congo River through Africa offered to speak to the gathering next Friday night

3. If only recent lesson of adversity proper manner they are lead useful honourable a successfully life

4. overlook property developed near Riverside Manor very much to offer before

Exercise 82

(Write in Shorthand)

Dear-Sirs, *We-are* afraid *that-we-shall-be* unable-*to* recover-*the* total sum due *on-your* claim unless *you* adopt *different* measures. *We-have* used *special* efforts, *but* up *to-the* present *we-have* met *with* no success *in-our* endeavours *to*-get-*the* debtor *to* settle. *We-are*-unable-*to* collect *any* money, *nor can-we* extract *any* promise *from-him*.

We-think-you-will-*be*-obliged finally *to* pass-*the* claim *over to-your* solicitors. Please notify us if-*you* wish-us *to* proceed *with-the* case *and* take *this* step *for-you*. *Very*-truly-*yours*, (100)

CHAPTER XII

46. N Hook

(a) A small final hook, written on the inside of curves, adds *n*—

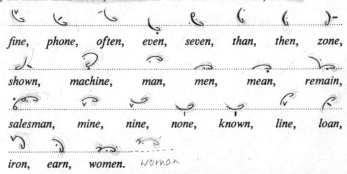

fine, phone, often, even, seven, than, then, zone,

shown, machine, man, men, mean, remain,

salesman, mine, nine, none, known, line, loan,

iron, earn, women. *woman*

(b) The *n* hook is written with a right (clockwise) motion at the end of all straight strokes—

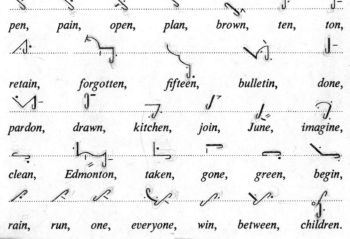

pen, pain, open, plan, brown, ten, ton,

retain, forgotten, fifteen, bulletin, done,

pardon, drawn, kitchen, join, June, imagine,

clean, Edmonton, taken, gone, green, begin,

rain, run, one, everyone, win, between, children.

Final *r*, when hooked, is usually written upward—

turn, return, learn, western, corn, pattern, Woburn.

SHORT FORMS

 been,   general or generally,   within,   southern,   northern,   opinion.

Phrases: had been,   have been,   more than,   better than, larger than,   smaller than,   our own,   their own,   going on,   carried on.

Exercise 83

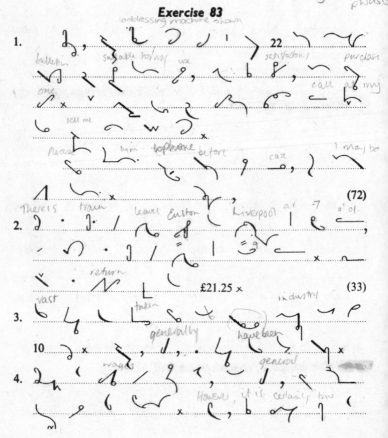

(72)

(33)

(10)

This page contains shorthand notation with interlinear longhand annotations.

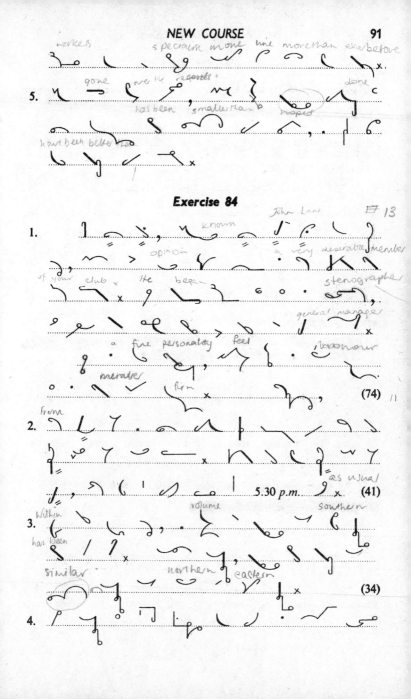

workers   s peciause in one line more than ever before

5. gone over the regards done c
has been smaller than hoped
have been better too

Exercise 84

1. John Lane 13
known
opinion a very desirable member
of your club He begin stenographer
general manager
a fine personality feel honour
member firm (74)

2. from
as usual
5.30 p.m. (41)

3. Within volume southern
has been similar northern eastern (34)

4.

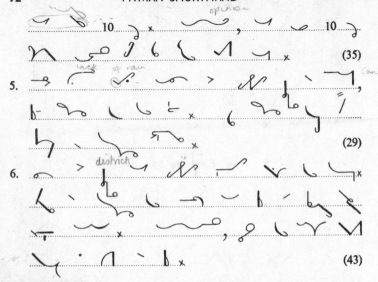

47. F or V Hook

(a) A small final hook, written with a left (anticlockwise) motion at the end of all straight strokes, adds *f* or *v*—

brief, proof or prove, approve, above, active, relative, attractive, drive, achieve, gave, rough, serve, deserve, preserve, reserve, wife, half.

(b) There is no *f* or *v* hook to curves.

SHORT FORMS

represent or represented, representative, behalf, advantage.

Phrases: out of, number of, instead of, which have, who have. you have

Exercise 85

1.

2.

3.

4.

(96)

Exercise 86

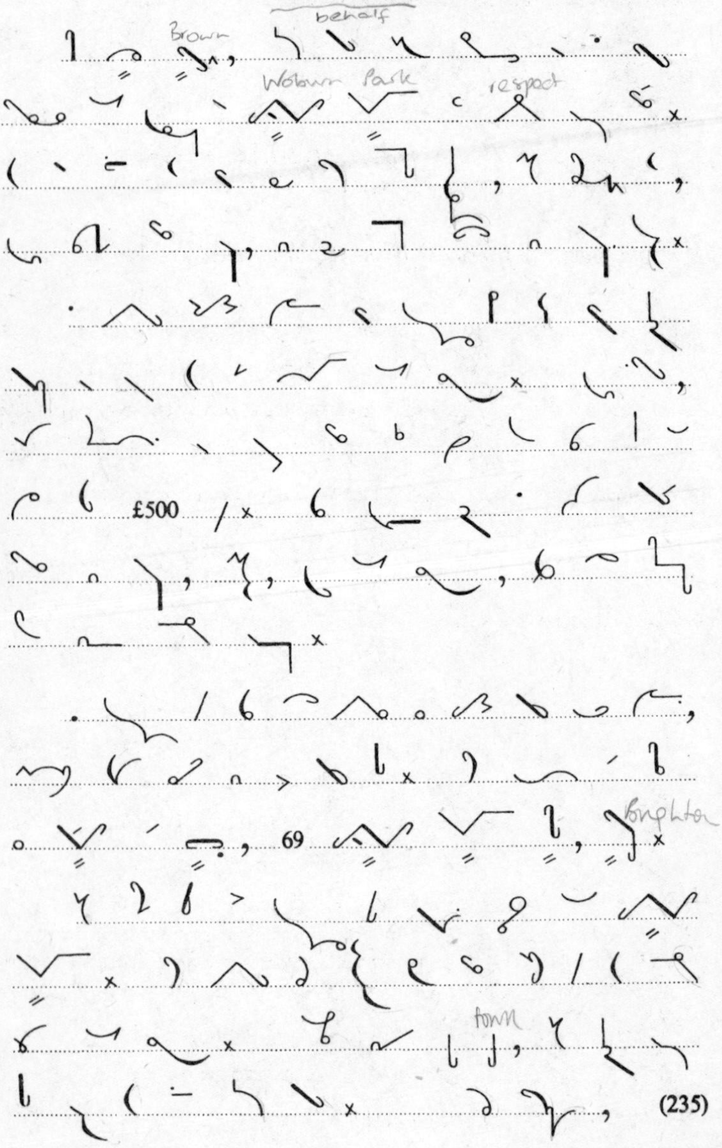
behalf
Brown
Woburn Park
respect
£500
69
Broughton
town
(235)

48. A finally hooked stroke is halved to indicate a following *t* or *d*—

(a) *find,   found,   event,   meant* or *mend,   demand,   mind,*

amount,   moment,   statement,   payment,   movement,   settlement,

shipment,   friend,   front,   department,   land,   around.

(b) *opened,   band,   print,   plant* or *planned,   spent* or *spend,   point,*

pound,   bound,   attend,   extent or *extend,   instant,   assistant,*

stand,   president,   kind,   count,   account,   discount,   second,

grand,   inclined,   went,   want,   turned,   current,   round,   returned.

(c) *approved,   gift,   served,   draft,   achieved,   deserved,*

reserved,   observed.

SHORT FORMS

gentleman,   gentlemen,   cannot,   told,   tried,
trade or *toward,   third.*

Phrases: *had not* or *do not,   did not.*

If it is necessary to indicate in your shorthand notes that a longhand abbreviation is to be used, write a fully vocalized outline for the abbreviation—

hadn't,   don't,   didn't,   doesn't,   haven't,
won't,   isn't,   couldn't,   can't.

NOTE: *can not* (separate words).

Exercise 87

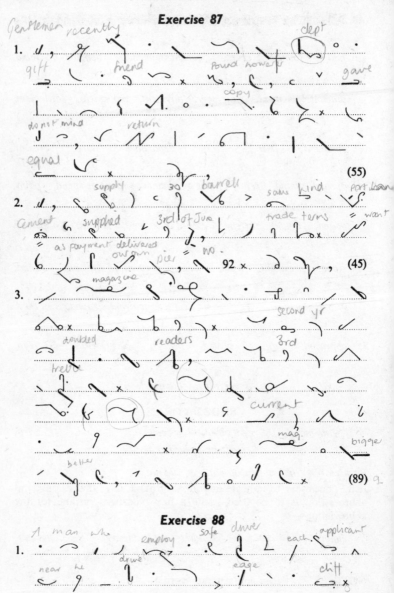

Exercise 88

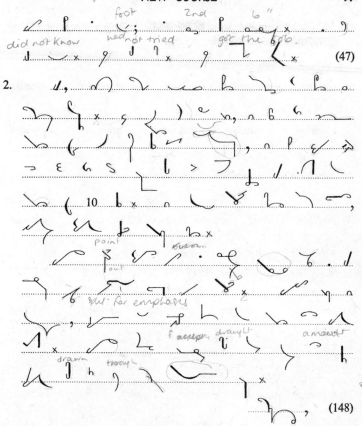

(47)

(148)

Exercise 89
(*Write in Shorthand*)

Gentlemen, Please *be* kind-enough *to* supply-*the* items *on-the* attached list *as*-soon-*as*-possible. At-*the* present moment *there-is* an active demand *for-them*, *and-we*-hope *that-we-can* count *on* hav*ing them within* three days. If-*you* find *that-you-cannot* supply *them within that*-time, please-*inform*-us by return.

Please-note-*that-the* exact items specified *are to-be* supplied. If-*you-are* out-*of* stock *of any of-the* items, *do*-not supply *different* articles. *Anything that-is*-not exactly *as* specified *should-be* returned. *Yours*-truly, (95)

49. Hooks for *v* and *n* are used in the middle of a word when they join easily to the following strokes— BALANCE OF OUTLINE

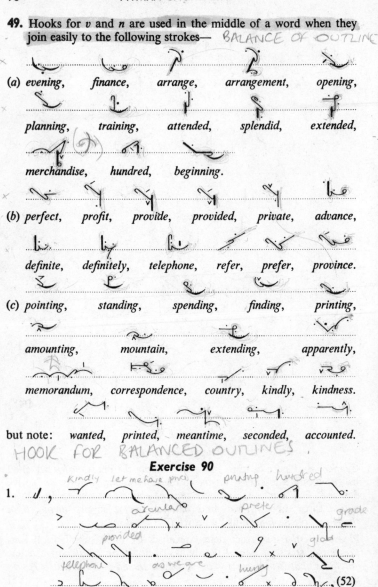

(a) *evening,   finance,   arrange,   arrangement,   opening,*

planning,   training,   attended,   splendid,   extended,

merchandise,   hundred,   beginning.

(b) *perfect,   profit,   provide,   provided,   private,   advance,*

definite,   definitely,   telephone,   refer,   prefer,   province.

(c) *pointing,   standing,   spending,   finding,   printing,*

amounting,   mountain,   extending,   apparently,

memorandum,   correspondence,   country,   kindly,   kindness.

but note: *wanted,   printed,   meantime,   seconded,   accounted.*

=> HOOK FOR BALANCED OUTLINES.

Exercise 90

1.   (52)

2. [shorthand outlines] *learn*

[shorthand outlines] *fancy* *apparently* *were enter* *printed* *or bound*

[shorthand outlines] *incorrectly,* *kindly return*

[shorthand outlines] *obtain* *credit*

[shorthand outlines]

[shorthand outlines] *plus*

[shorthand outlines] (68)

Exercise 91

stenography [shorthand outlines] *a* *one hundred percent* *subj* *of mean*

achieve *perfect accuracy* [shorthand outlines] *use*

office *remember* [shorthand outlines] *men* *want*

appear [shorthand outlines] *correspondance* [shorthand outlines]

You must be able to [shorthand outlines] *perfect*

arranged [shorthand outlines]

strive *will* *sure* *advance* [shorthand outlines]
develop habit *accuracy* *from beginning* *training* (95)

Exercise 92

planning [shorthand outlines] *sale* *home furnishings* *during* *Oct.*

open stocks [shorthand outlines] *next* *to*

husband + wife [shorthand outlines]

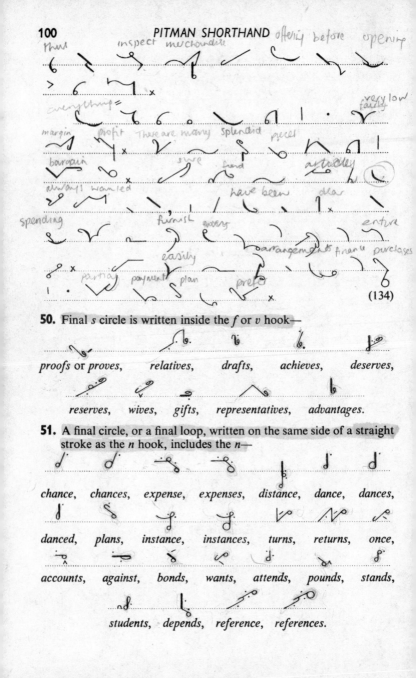

50. Final *s* circle is written inside the *f* or *v* hook—

proofs or proves,   relatives,   drafts,   achieves,   deserves,

reserves,   wives,   gifts,   representatives,   advantages.

51. A final circle, or a final loop, written on the same side of a straight stroke as the *n* hook, includes the *n*—

chance,   chances,   expense,   expenses,   distance,   dance,   dances,

danced,   plans,   instance,   instances,   turns,   returns,   once,

accounts,   against,   bonds,   wants,   attends,   pounds,   stands,

students,   depends,   reference,   references.

52. A circle written inside an *n* hook attached to a full-length curve adds the final sound *z* only—

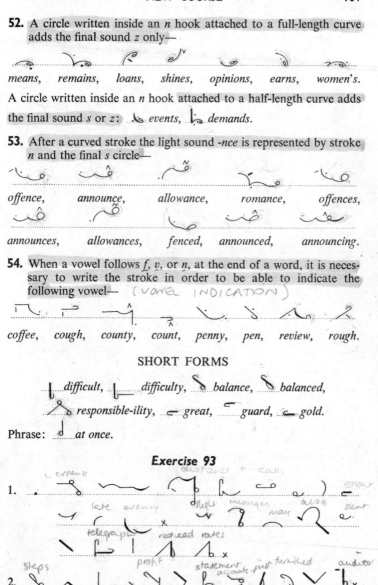

means,   remains,   loans,   shines,   opinions,   earns,   women's.

A circle written inside an *n* hook attached to a half-length curve adds the final sound *s* or *z*:   *events,*   *demands.*

53. After a curved stroke the light sound *-nce* is represented by stroke *n* and the final *s* circle—

offence,   announce,   allowance,   romance,   offences,

announces,   allowances,   fenced,   announced,   announcing.

54. When a vowel follows *f, v,* or *n,* at the end of a word, it is necessary to write the stroke in order to be able to indicate the following vowel—   (VOWEL INDICATION)

coffee,   cough,   county,   count,   penny,   pen,   review,   rough.

SHORT FORMS

difficult,   difficulty,   balance,   balanced,

responsible-ility,   great,   guard,   gold.

Phrase: *at once.*

Exercise 93

1.

2.

it has been found *necessary* *reduce* *in our plan* *clear*

3.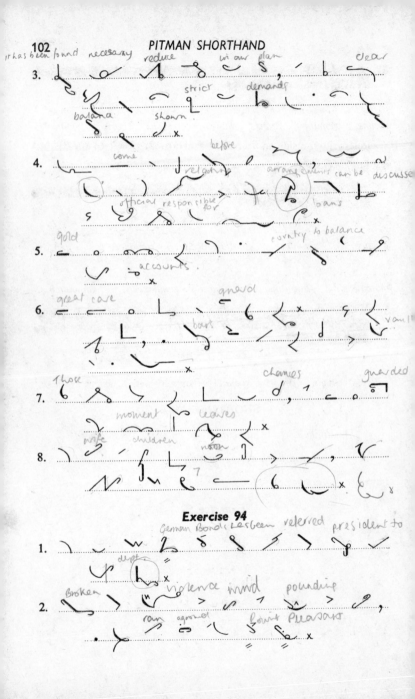

strict *demands*

balance *shown*

come *before*

4. *relation* *arrangements can be discussed*

official responsible for *loans*

gold

5. *country to balance*

accounts.

great care *guard*

6. *van !!*

bars

Those *changes* *guarded*

7.

moment *leaves*

wife *children* *noon*

8.

Exercise 94

German Bonds *has been* *referred* *president to*

1.

dept.

Broken *violence* *mind* *pounding*

2.

ran *against* *Mount Pleasant*

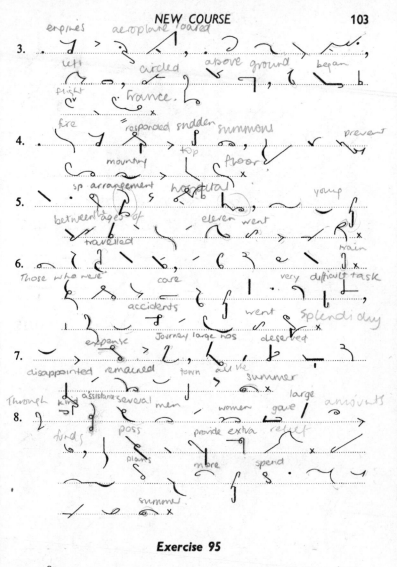

3. [shorthand outlines with annotations: engines, aeroplane, roared, left, circled, above ground, began, flight, France]

4. [shorthand outlines: fire, responded, sudden, summons, prevent, mountain, top, floor]

5. [shorthand outlines: sp arrangement, hospital, young, between ages of, eleven, went, travelled]

6. [shorthand outlines: train, Those who were, care, very difficult task, accidents, went, Splendidly]

7. [shorthand outlines: expense, Journey, large nos, deserted, disappointed, remained, town, all the, summer]

8. [shorthand outlines: Through, kind, assistance, several men, women, gave, large, amounts, funds, poss, provide extra relief, plans, more, spend, summer]

Exercise 95

[shorthand outlines]

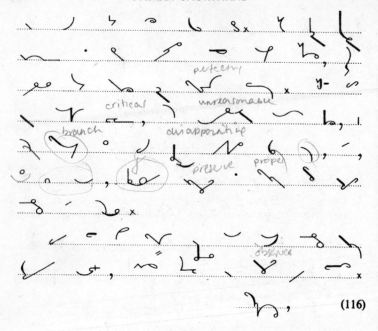

(116)

Exercise 96

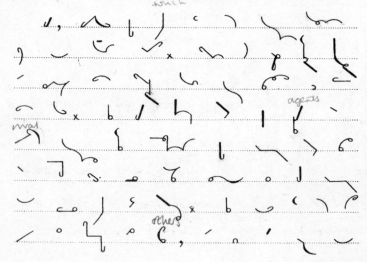

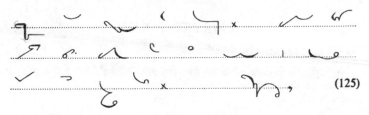

(125)

Exercise 97

(*Write in Shorthand*)

1. *This* firm gave us excellent references, so *we-think-we should* extend-*the* time *for*-payment *of-the balance* due *on-their*-account.

2. *The young*-man stands *a very*-good chance *of* obtaining-*the* post *of* assistant manager *of-the* bond department *owing to-the* splendid training he-*has* received.

3. Please provide us *with a* memorandum *of all* merchandise *which-is subject to a special* allowance.

4. *The* rough draft serves *to* show *how-the* use *of-the* telephone *has-been* extended *during-the* last seven *years*.

5. *Several of-the* students *have-been* taken out-*of-the* second grade, *and-we* plan *to*-make other arrangements *for-those-who* remain.

6. *Your* statement *is* returned *because-the* amount *of-the* discount *that-you have* deducted *is*-not correct.

Exercise 98

(*Write in Shorthand*)

Gentlemen, We should-be ungrateful indeed if-*we*-did-not accept *your* kind hint. *As a* direct result *we-have* planned *a* series *of* trips *for our representatives which*-will bring *them* into closer touch *with our* customers *all-over-the* country. *Our* men *are* leaving at-once *with* samples *of-our* advance lines. They-will explain *to-you-the* reasons *for-the* apparent slackness *we-have* shown *during-the* past season. *It-has-been* one *of-much* stress *for*-us, *and-we-are*-inclined-*to-think* you-will make-*the* proper allowances *when-you* learn-*the* reason.

You-will-*be*-glad *to* know *that-the* new lines *to-be* shown *to-you* have-*been* favourably received *in-the* east. They-*are of* splendid value, *and are* sold at-prices *that give*-us *a very*-low margin *of*-profit. *Yours very*-truly, (144)

CHAPTER XIII

55. -Shun Hook

A large final hook adds the final syllable *-shun*. This large hook is written on the inside of curves—

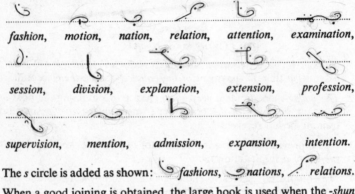

fashion,   motion,   nation,   relation,   attention,   examination,

session,   division,   explanation,   extension,   profession,

supervision,   mention,   admission,   expansion,   intention.

The *s* circle is added as shown: fashions, nations, relations.

When a good joining is obtained, the large hook is used when the *-shun* syllable occurs in the middle of a word—

national,   professional,   intentional.

Exercise 99

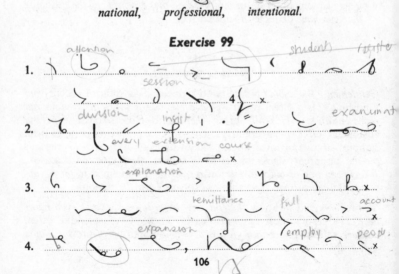

1.

2.

3.

4.

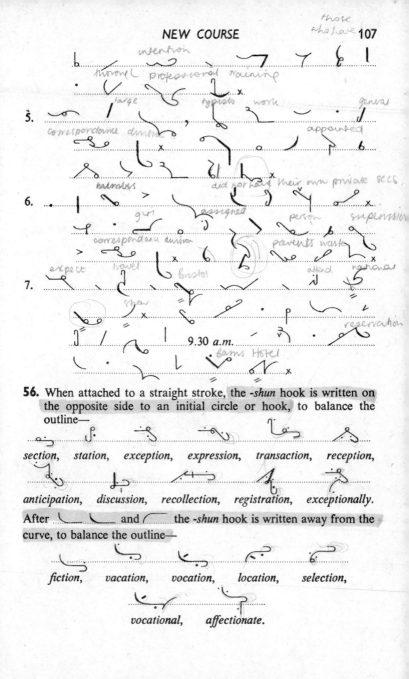

56. When attached to a straight stroke, the *-shun* hook is written on the opposite side to an initial circle or hook, to balance the outline—

section, station, exception, expression, transaction, reception,

anticipation, discussion, recollection, registration, exceptionally.

After ⌒ ⌒ and ⌒ the *-shun* hook is written away from the curve, to balance the outline—

fiction, vacation, vocation, location, selection,

vocational, affectionate.

Exercise 100

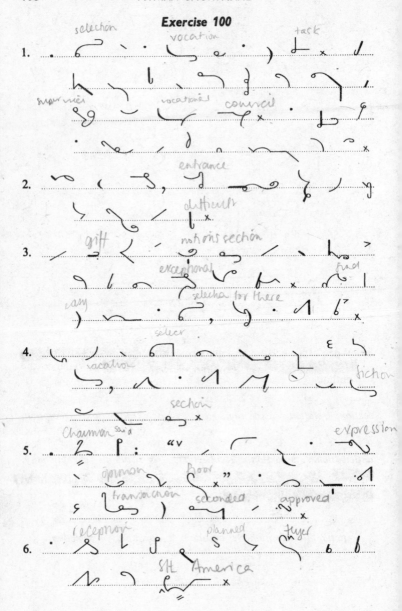

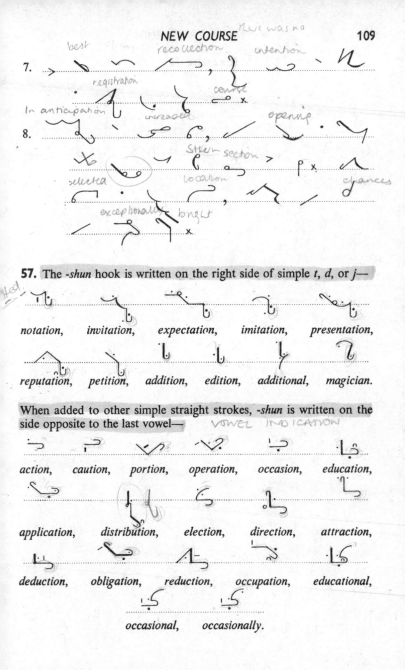

7.

8.

57. The *-shun* hook is written on the right side of simple *t*, *d*, or *j*—

notation,   invitation,   expectation,   imitation,   presentation,

reputation,   petition,   addition,   edition,   additional,   magician.

When added to other simple straight strokes, *-shun* is written on the side opposite to the last vowel—

action,   caution,   portion,   operation,   occasion,   education,

application,   distribution,   election,   direction,   attraction,

deduction,   obligation,   reduction,   occupation,   educational,

occasional,   occasionally.

Exercise 101

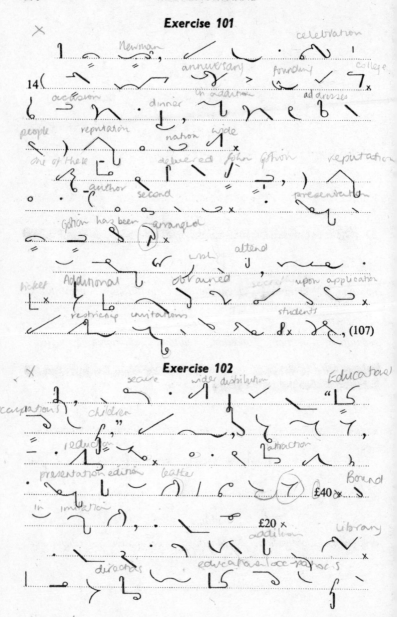

(107)

Exercise 102

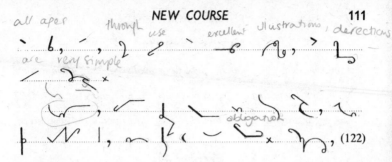

58. S-Shun

When *-shun* follows the *s* circle or the *ns* circle, it is represented by a small curl (a continuation of the circle). A third-place vowel between the *s* and *-shun* is placed outside the curl. Any other vowel is not indicated.

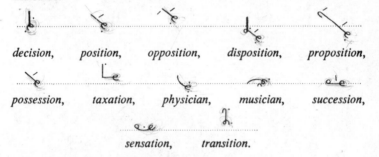

decision, position, opposition, disposition, proposition,

possession, taxation, physician, musician, succession,

sensation, transition.

A final *s* circle is placed inside the curl—

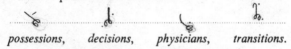

possessions, decisions, physicians, transitions.

59. In words ending in *-uation* or *-uition*, the stroke *sh* and *n* hook are generally used—

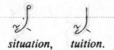

situation, tuition.

A stroke hooked for *-shun* is halved to indicate a final *t* or *d*—

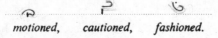

motioned, cautioned, fashioned.

SHORT FORMS

⌇ information,   public, publish or published,   publication,
object or objected,   objection,   organize or organized,
organization, satisfaction, investigation, yesterday.

Exercise 103

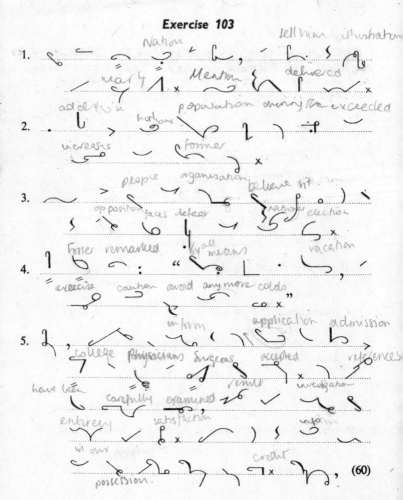

(60)

Exercise 104

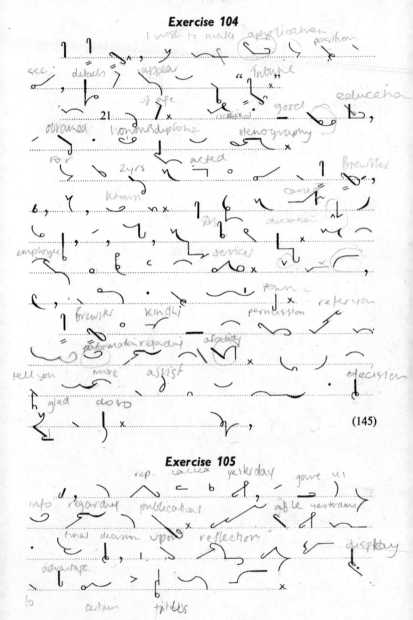

(145)

Exercise 105

(shorthand outlines with longhand annotations)

deliver   at once   dozen   copies   each

Dictionary   of   Education

Public Finance   ;   Corporation Law

objection

And does not   save   readily

keep us   informed   books

by your organisation.

(98)

Exercise 106

because of   decision   build

position   next year

permit   occasion   courtesies

extended

Preparations   erection   offices   salesrooms

there is just a chance

building may not   lease   with

provision   delays   subject

yr permission   building if necessary

not more than   remain

objection   arrangement

(133)

Exercise 107

(*Write in Shorthand*)

Gentlemen, We-think-we-are in *a* position *to* assist *you to-tell in what* direction *your* promotion work may best *be* extended. *As you-are-*no-doubt aware, *our organization has given* many *years of* attention *to* problems *of* distribution *of-*every *description, and-the information in-our-*possession *is very* reliable.

*We-believe-that-you would-*find *a* discussion *of-the* problem *with our Mr.* Jones *of-*value *to-you.* He-will-*be-*glad *to-*receive *an* invitation *from-you to-call. Very-*truly-*yours,* (87)

Exercise 108

(*Write in Shorthand*)

*Dear-*Sir, *With-the* small amount *of information in-our-*possession, *we-are-*unable-*to give-you a* definite decision *on-your* application *for a* loan. *You-*make no mention at-*all of any* provision *for* expansion at-*your* present factory, *nor do-you tell-*us if-*you have any* intention *of-*taking *over-the* operation *of more* machines.

However, we-believe-that-the proposition *is* certainly worth discussion, *although* action must, *of-*course, wait *till-you* supply us *with* additional *information* about *your* plans.

*We-*suggest *that-you call* at-*our* office some time *during-the-next* few days, *to-*permit us *to-*go *over* every detail *of-the* situation *with-you.* *Yours-*truly, (114)

CHAPTER XIV

60. Compound Consonants

Besides the double consonants in the *pel* and *per* series, there are six compound consonants—

Letter	Sign	Name	As in
KW		kwa	quick, request
GW		gwa	Guelph, linguist
MP, MB		emp } emb }	camp, embody
LR		ler	filler, scholar
RR		rer	poorer, sharer
WH		hwa	where, whip

NOTE: *Ler* is used only where the downward *l* would be used; *rer* is used only where the downward *r* would be used. *(Can be brought down)*

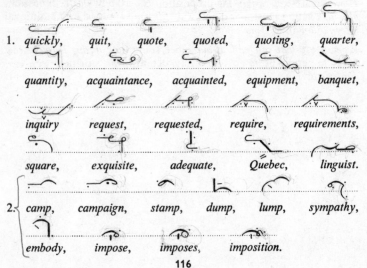

1. quickly, quit, quote, quoted, quoting, quarter,

quantity, acquaintance, acquainted, equipment, banquet,

inquiry request, requested, require, requirements,

square, exquisite, adequate, Quebec, linguist.

2. camp, campaign, stamp, dump, lump, sympathy,

embody, impose, imposes, imposition.

116

3. *roller,   counsellor,   ruler,   scholars.*

4. *bearer,   fairer,   admirer,   poorer,   sharer,   wearer.*

5. *white,   anywhere,   nowhere,   everywhere,   elsewhere.*

When *m* is immediately followed by *pr, br, pl,* or *bl,* the double consonant strokes are used—

impress,   embrace,   imply,   emblem.

SHORT FORMS

*whether, *important or importance, *improve, improved or improvement, *impossible, *child, *chaired, *cheered, *accord or according (or according to), *cared, *particular, *opportunity.*

Phrases: *according to, *according to the.*

Exercise 109

1.

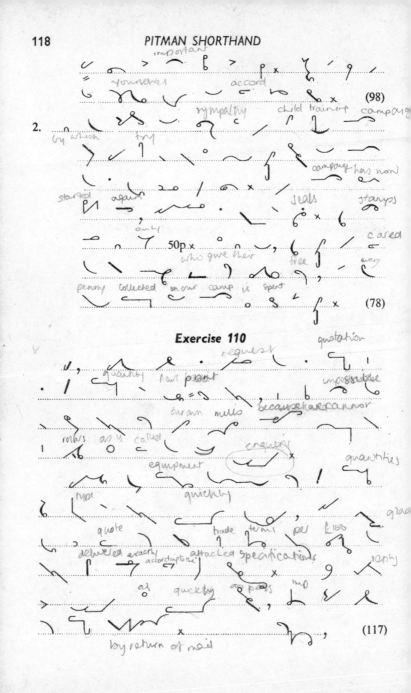

(98)

2. ...

(78)

Exercise 110

(117)

Exercise 111

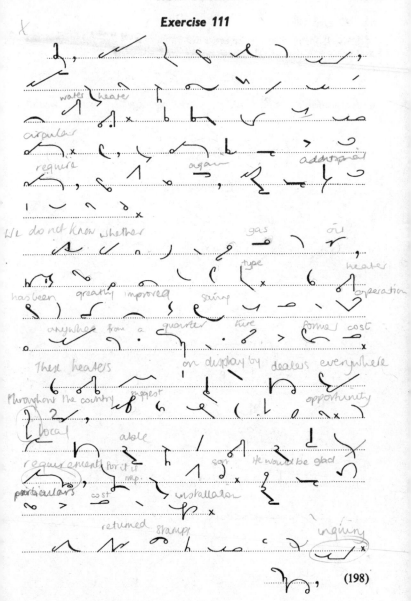

(198)

61. Wl and Whl

A small initial hook prefixes *w* to upward *l*. A large initial hook prefixes *wh* to upward *l*. These hooks are read first—

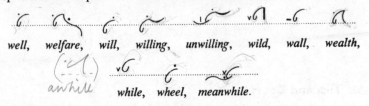

well, welfare, will, willing, unwilling, wild, wall, wealth, anwhile, while, wheel, meanwhile.

Exercise 112

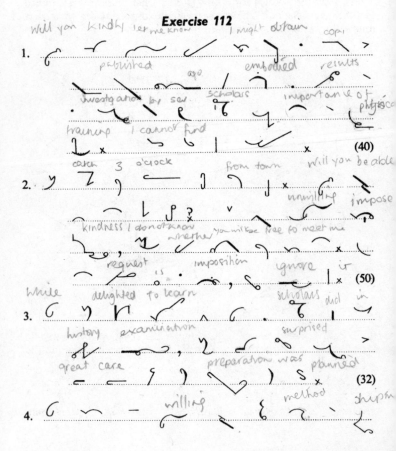

1. Will you kindly let me know I might obtain copy published ago embodied results investigation by say scholars importance of physical training I cannot find (40)

2. catch 3 o'clock from town Will you be able unwilling impose kindness I do not know whether you will be free to meet me request imposition ignore it (50)

3. while delighted to learn scholars did in history examination surprised great care preparation was planned (32)

4. willing method shipm

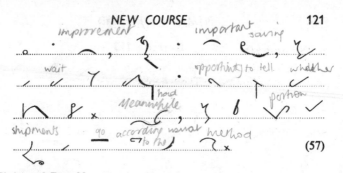

(handwritten annotations: improvement, important, saving, wait, opportunity to tell, whether, Meanwhile, hard, portion, shipments, go accordingly usual method, according to the)

(57)

62. Tick and Dot H

Generally the upward form of *h* is used when this stroke is joined to other consonants. When *h* is the only consonant, or when it is followed by *k* or *g*, the downward form is used—

he, hug, hog, hook, high, highway.

(a) The upward form is used for half-length *h* standing alone—

hate, hot, hat, heat, height.

(b) A small tick, written as shown, represents *h* before *m*, *l*, and downward *r*— *(HOMELIER) (only when h is first, no vowel)*

home, whom, Hamilton, hall, health, hello,

help, hold, holiday, hair, hear or here, her,

herself, horse, hurt, harm.

(c) Where it would be awkward to write the stroke *h* in the middle of a word, *h* is represented by a light dot placed alongside the vowel sound, in words such as—

perhaps, neighbourhood, likelihood, household, Manhattan.

also propose,
so dots help)

Exercise 113

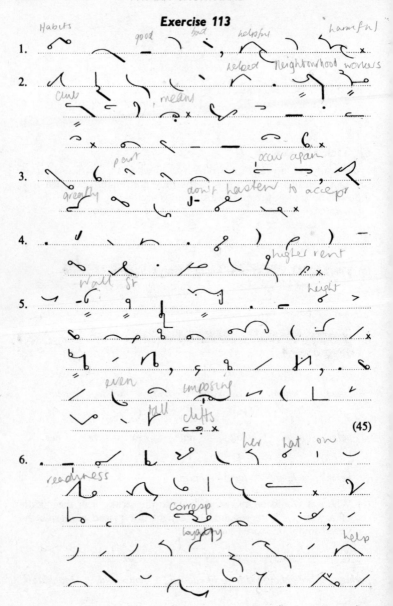

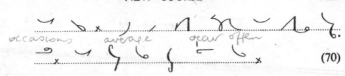

occasions   average   occur often

(70)

63. Omission of Consonants

(a) Where a medial *t* is only lightly sounded after circle *s*, it may sometimes be omitted, as in—

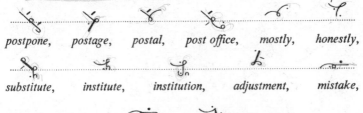

postpone,   postage,   postal,   post office,   mostly,   honestly,

substitute,   institute,   institution,   adjustment,   mistake,

mistaken,   investigate.

(b) Other lightly sounded consonants may sometimes be omitted, as in—

anxious,   anxiously,   distinct,   distinction,   prompt,   stamped.

Exercise 114

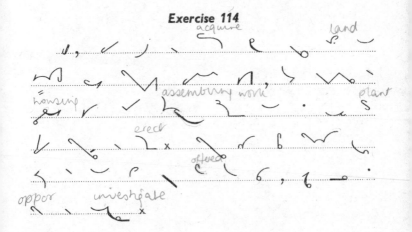

acquire   land   housing   assembly   work   plant   erect   offered   oppor   investigate

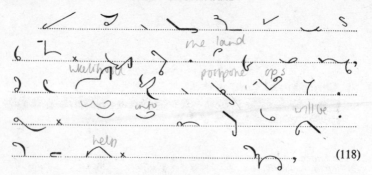

(118)

Exercise 115

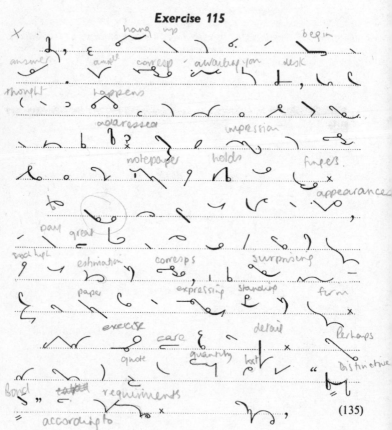

(135)

Exercise 116

(*Write in Shorthand*)

1. *Gentlemen, We-are* anxious *to*-receive-*the* pens *which according-to your* invoice *of* 14th-*November* were *sent* by post five days ago. *We*-presume *that-the* parcel *was sent* by registered post.

   In-answer *to-our* inquiry, *the* post-office here says *that-the* package *has*-not-yet-*been* received. *Do-you think that-there-has-been* a mistake *in* addressing-*it*? *Yours very*-truly, (66)

2. *Gentlemen, We-are*-sorry *to*-learn *that-the* package *we-sent to-you* by registered post *on* 14th-*November has*-not-*been* received. Promptly upon receipt *of-your* note *we-sent* a duplicate. *It-is*-possible, *of*-course, *that-the* label *was* incorrectly addressed, *but-we-do*-not-*think that-there-is* any likelihood *that-this-is-the* case. *We-are* asking-*the* postal authorities *to* institute a search *for-the* lost parcel, *and*-no-doubt they-will-*be*-able-*to* find *it*.

   Meanwhile, if-*the* original package *is delivered to-you*, will-*you*-kindly return *it to*-us. *The* cost *of* postage will-*be-sent to-you*, or *you-can* make *an* adjustment *in-your*-account *when-you* post *your* cheque. *Very*-truly-*yours*, (125)

CHAPTER XV

64. Halving

There are a few additional applications of the halving principle.

(a) The strokes *m* and *n* are halved and thickened to indicate a following *d*—

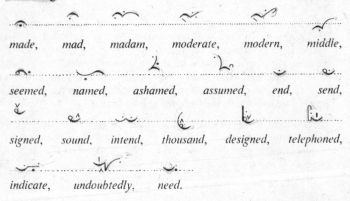

made,   mad,   madam,   moderate,   modern,   middle,

seemed,   named,   ashamed,   assumed,   end,   send,

signed,   sound,   intend,   thousand,   designed,   telephoned,

indicate,   undoubtedly,   need.

(b) Downward *l* and downward *r* are halved and thickened to indicate a following *d*—

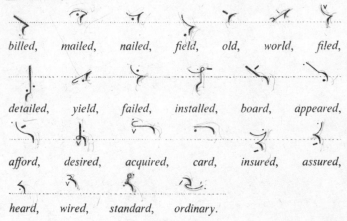

billed,   mailed,   nailed,   field,   old,   world,   filed,

detailed,   yield,   failed,   installed,   board,   appeared,

afford,   desired,   acquired,   card,   insured,   assured,

heard,   wired,   standard,   ordinary.

Exercise 117

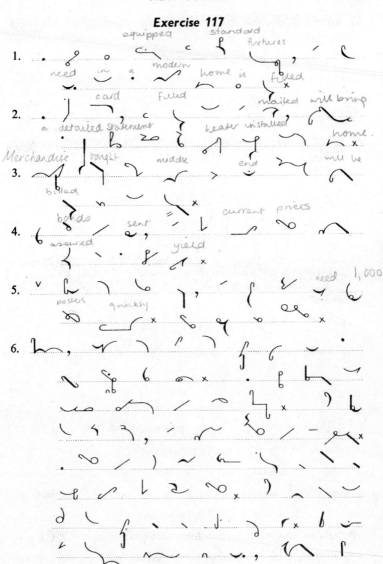

(95)

65. Final *lt* is expressed by ⌒ , and final *rt* is generally expressed by ╱ —

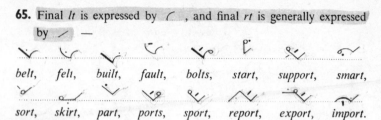

belt,   felt,   built,   fault,   bolts,   start,   support,   smart,

sort,   skirt,   part,   ports,   sport,   report,   export,   import.

66. When a vowel comes between *l-d* or *r-d*, the full strokes must be written—

carried,   delayed,   followed,   married,   valued,

borrowed,   worried.

67. As indicated in paragraph 35 (*b*), strokes of unequal length must not be joined if their length would not clearly show. To show the difference in length, disjoin half-length *t* or *d* following stroke *t* or *d*—

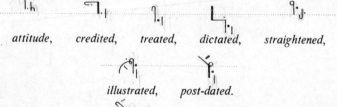

attitude,   credited,   treated,   dictated,   straightened,

illustrated,   post-dated.

Special use of disjoining: ⌇ *promptness,* ⌇ *indebtedness,* │ *outfit.*

SHORT FORMS

⟋ *short,* ⌒ *hand,* ⌣ *under,* ⟍ *yard,* ⟍ *word,* ⌢ *immediate,*

⌒ *school,* ⌒ *schooled,* ⌒ *spirit,* ⌒ *certificate,* ⟍ *knowledge,*

⟍ *acknowledge.*

The halving principle is used to form such phrases as ⌣ *if it,* ⌣ *if it is,*

⟍ *in which it is,* ⟍ *I am not,* ⌒ *you are not,* ⌒ *you will not,*

⌣ *you were not,* ⌣ *this would be,* ⌣ *I would.*

Exercise 118

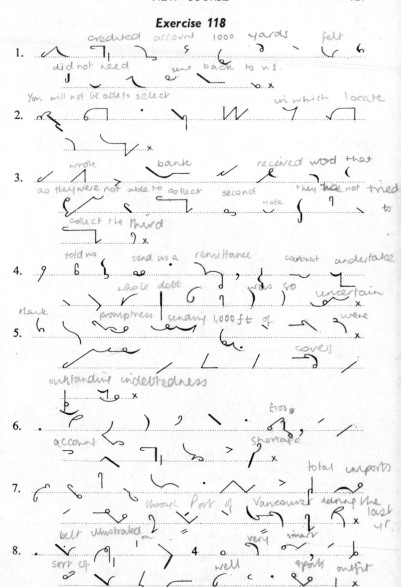

Exercise 119

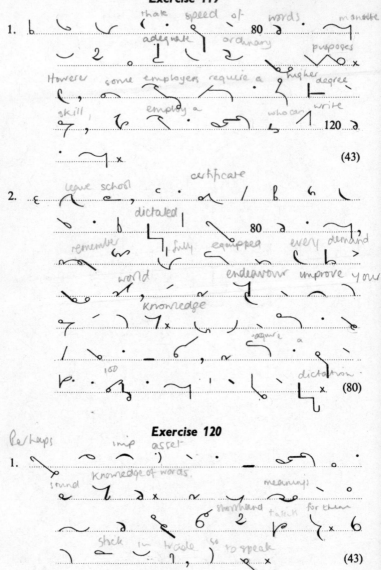

1. that speed of words. minute
80
adequate ordinary purposes
However some employers require a higher degree
skill, employ a who can write 120
(43)

2. leave school, certificate
dictated
80
remember, fully equipped every demand
word, endeavour improve your
knowledge
acquire a
150
dictation (80)

Exercise 120

1. Perhaps imp asset
sound knowledge of words.
meanings
shorthand talent for them
stick in trade, so to speak
(43)

2. *[shorthand outlines]* ... of encourage knowledge of words and shorthand skill read articles dictated from a newspaper magazine did not know meanings dictionary immediately can do this at once place a circle around these words & find out their meanings when an opp. presents itself very good way to increase knowledge of s.h. outlines (65)

3. *[shorthand outlines]* is to read plenty of literature written in s.h. Always be sure to look up the meanings of any words you do not understand (35)

Exercise 121

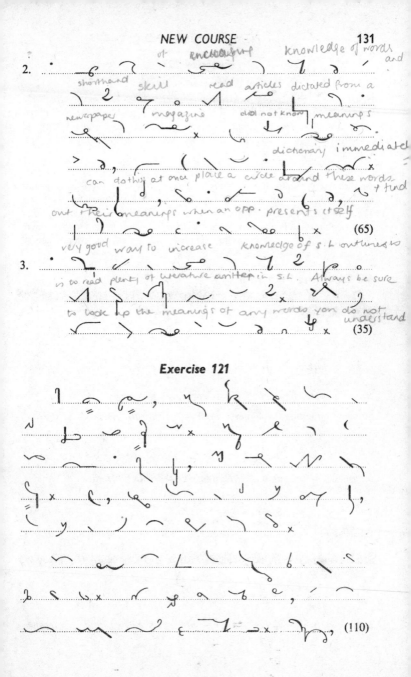

(110)

Exercise 122

(Write in Shorthand)

Gentlemen, Please-*inform*-us *immediately when-we*-may *expect-the* lighting fixtures *we* ordered *from-you* on 7th October, *for-the* apartment house *we-are*-now *building.* *According-to* our *under*standing at *that*-time, *you*-were *to-deliver* them *towards-the* end *of-the*-month, *but-you have* failed *to do*-so.

*It-is under*stood, *of*-course, *that-the* delay may not *be* intentional *on-your* part, *but-we-have* received no *word from-you.* Please-*do*-not hesitate *to inform*-us *if-you-are*-not able-*to-make* *immediate delivery.* *We-think-you*-will-not mis*under*stand *our* attitude *when-we* say *that if-you-cannot deliver-them immediately we-shall-have to*-get *them* elsewhere. Work *is*-now *being* delayed, *and-we* simply *cannot* afford *to*-wait. *Very*-truly-*yours,*   (131)

68. Doubling Principle

Curved strokes are doubled in length to indicate a following syllable *tr, dr,* or *THr*— *(ture)*

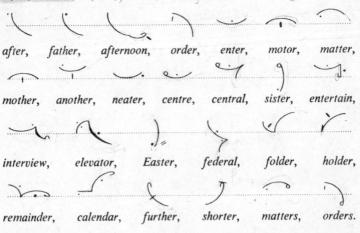

after,   father,   afternoon,   order,   enter,   motor,   matter,

mother,   another,   neater,   centre,   central,   sister,   entertain,

interview,   elevator,   Easter,   federal,   folder,   holder,

remainder,   calendar,   further,   shorter,   matters,   orders.

Stroke *l* standing alone, or with only a final *s* circle, is doubled to add *tr* only—

letter,   letters,   later,   latter,   alter, but *leader,*   older,   leather.

Exercise 123

Exercise 124

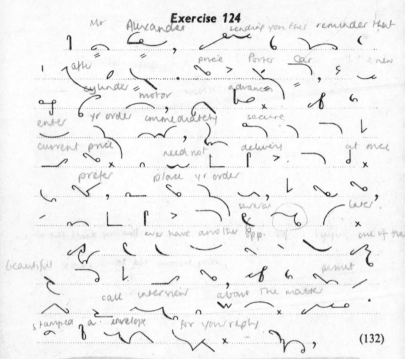

(132)

69. A straight stroke is doubled to indicate *tr*, *dr*, or *THr*, only—
  (1) when it follows another stroke or circle *s*, or
  (2) when it has a finally joined diphthong or a final hook—

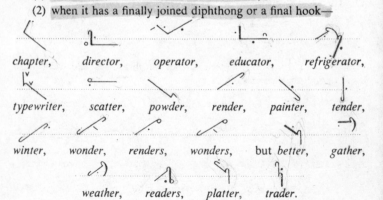

chapter, director, operator, educator, refrigerator,

typewriter, scatter, powder, render, painter, tender,

winter, wonder, renders, wonders, but *better*, gather,

weather, readers, platter, trader.

70. In a few common words the syllable *-ture* is represented by the doubling principle—

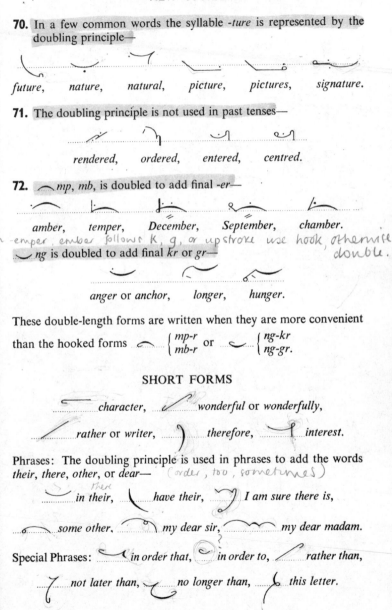

future,   nature,   natural,   picture,   pictures,   signature.

71. The doubling principle is not used in past tenses—

rendered,   ordered,   entered,   centred.

72. ⌒ *mp, mb,* is doubled to add final *-er—*

amber,   temper,   December,   September,   chamber.

n -emper, ember follows K, g, or upstroke use hook, otherwise double.

⌣ *ng* is doubled to add final *kr* or *gr—*

anger or anchor,   longer,   hunger.

These double-length forms are written when they are more convenient

than the hooked forms ⌒ { mp-r / mb-r } or ⌣ { ng-kr / ng-gr }.

SHORT FORMS

.... character, ... wonderful or wonderfully,

.... rather or writer, ... therefore, ... interest.

Phrases: The doubling principle is used in phrases to add the words *their, there, other,* or *dear—* *(order, too, sometimes)*

.... in their, ... have their, *there*   .... I am sure there is,

.... some other, ... my dear sir, ... my dear madam.

Special Phrases: .... in order that, ... in order to, ... rather than,

.... not later than, ... no longer than, ... this letter.

Exercise 125

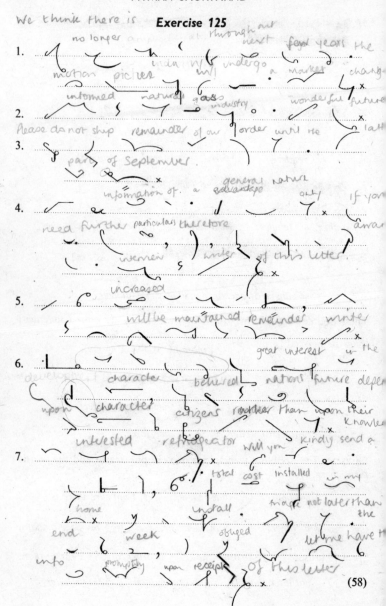

We think there is

1. no longer any ... at though our next few years the motion picture will undergo a marked change. informed natural gass

2. industry. wonderful future

Please do not ship remainder of our order until the latt

3. part of September.

information of a general nature
advantage only if you

4. need further particulars therefore aware interview winter of this letter.

increased

5. will be maintained remainder winter

great interest in the

6. development character believed nations future depend upon character citizens rather than upon their knowle

interested refrigerator will you kindly send a

7. total cost installed in my home install made not later than the end week obliged let me have the into promptly upon receipt of this letter

(58)

8.

invention > typewriter shorthand a₁ very valuable

art in order to demands of the bs. world

to be an accurate write 2 skilful operator

> two subjects

twin arts x.

The object shorthand training enable

dictation so that write matter dictated rapidly x.

in order that you may acquire degree of skill

within from your notes, the letters

or other matter dictated lessons as fast as

vo possibly can x.

(103)

Exercise 126

motor scooters

making their way of our country has been rapidly

increasing, method of travelling.

great future x motor scooter in many cases

replaced bicycle of earlier days 'cos it is swifter and

smarter x supporters esp, remote/

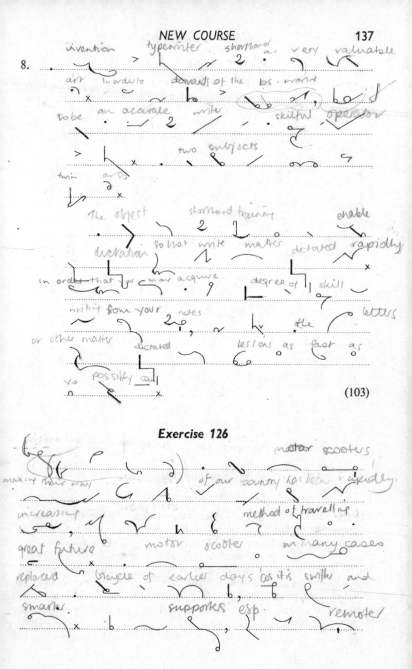

[Shorthand outlines with interlinear longhand annotations:]

districts out of the way railways where represents

means of bringing people closer touch centres

size the motor scooter render

it easy to manage on narrow roads many people are favourable

disposed towards it feature can be better understood if we

picture vehicle seeking pass scooter

narrow

Those who object to motor scooter do in their opinion

motor scooters are adding amount traffic

on our roads. But the scooter is safer and less noisy than

motor cycle and will be by more and more

people future

(188)

Exercise 127

(*Write in Shorthand*)

My-*dear*-Sir, *On behalf of*-*our*-clients, Messrs. Cantor *and* Walters, *who-have* requested us *to-represent their interests in-the*-matter *of-the* leasehold *on-the building* at 129 Wharf Street, *we-wish to inform-you that-we-have-their* permission *to* obtain *a* court order, *under-the* terms *of-which you*-will-not-*be*-able-*to* alter *the* front *of-the building*. *We-think-there-is* no-doubt *that-the*-terms *of-the* lease *have-been* violated, *and in-our-opinion it*-will-*be to-your interest to* stop *any* further operations until *a* decision *has-been* rendered by-*the* court. *Very*-truly-*yours*,   (108)

CHAPTER XVI

73. Prefixes

(a) The prefix *con-*, or *com-*, is expressed by a dot, written first at the beginning of an outline, as shown. In words beginning with the *con-* or *com-* dot, the first vowel after the prefix determines the position of the outline—

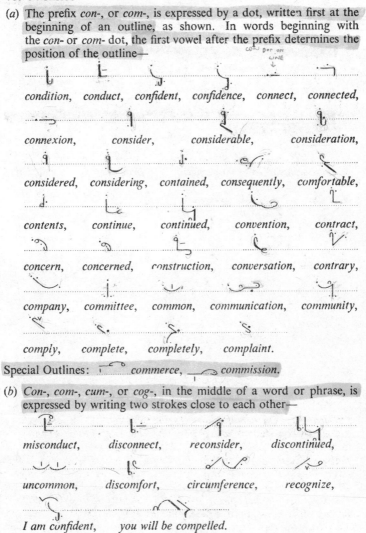

condition, conduct, confident, confidence, connect, connected,

connexion, consider, considerable, consideration,

considered, considering, contained, consequently, comfortable,

contents, continue, continued, convention, contract,

concern, concerned, construction, conversation, contrary,

company, committee, common, communication, community,

comply, complete, completely, complaint.

Special Outlines: commerce, commission.

(b) *Con-*, *com-*, *cum-*, or *cog-*, in the middle of a word or phrase, is expressed by writing two strokes close to each other—

misconduct, disconnect, reconsider, discontinued,

uncommon, discomfort, circumference, recognize,

I am confident, you will be compelled.

139

74. (a) *Accom-* or *accommo-* is expressed by _____ k, either joined or disjoined (always in the first position)—

All 1st vowel of prefix

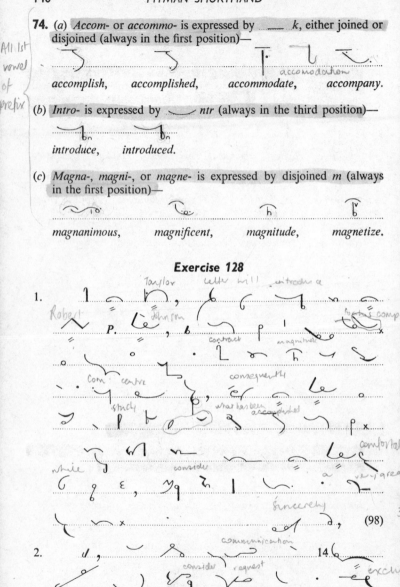

accomplish, accomplished, accommodate, accompany.

(b) *Intro-* is expressed by _____ ntr (always in the third position)—

introduce, introduced.

(c) *Magna-*, *magni-*, or *magne-* is expressed by disjoined *m* (always in the first position)—

magnanimous, magnificent, magnitude, magnetize.

Exercise 128

1.

(98)

2. 14

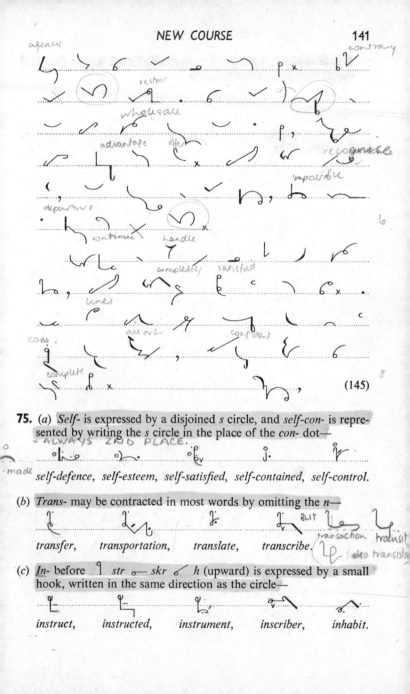

75. (a) *Self-* is expressed by a disjoined *s* circle, and *self-con-* is represented by writing the *s* circle in the place of the *con-* dot—

self-defence, self-esteem, self-satisfied, self-contained, self-control.

(b) *Trans-* may be contracted in most words by omitting the *n*—

transfer,   transportation,   translate,   transcribe.

(c) *In-* before ⌐ *str* ↄ *skr* ⌐ *h* (upward) is expressed by a small hook, written in the same direction as the circle—

instruct,   instructed,   instrument,   inscriber,   inhabit.

(d) Negative Words. When the prefix *in-* means *not*, it is always expressed by the stroke *n*, as in—

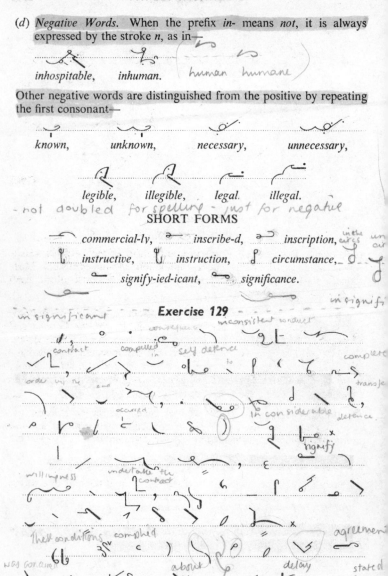

inhospitable, inhuman. *(human humane)*

Other negative words are distinguished from the positive by repeating the first consonant—

known, unknown, necessary, unnecessary,

legible, illegible, legal. illegal.

- not doubled for spelling - just for negative

SHORT FORMS

commercial-ly, inscribe-d, inscription,

instructive, instruction, circumstance,

signify-ied-icant, significance.

Exercise 129

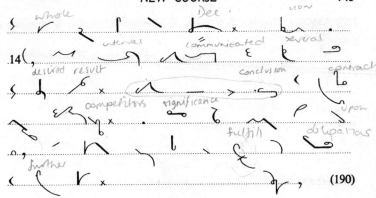

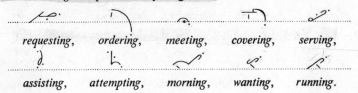

(190)

Exercise 130

(Write in Shorthand)

Gentlemen, We-received *your* communication *of-the* 14th, *in-which-you* complain *of-the* delay *in-the* completion *of-your* contract. *That-we-have* failed *to* accomplish *what we*-promised *we*-must admit, *and-we very*-much regret *our* failure.

We-are confident, *however, that-the* contract *could-have-been* completed *as* agreed upon *but for-the* recent trouble *with-the Commercial* Transport Committee, *which-was immediate*ly *responsible for-the* delay. *Their* decision interfered considerably *with our* business, *and-when-we* state *that* only thirty *of-our* transport men *have* continued at work, *we-think-you*-will recognize *how difficult it-has-been to* satisfy *our* customers.

It-is-unnecessary *for*-us *to* add *that-we should* regret-*the* transfer *of-your* business, considering-*the* long connexion between us, *and-the* cause *of-the* present interruption. *Very*-truly-*yours,* (139)

76. Suffixes and Word-endings

Where it would be awkward to write ⌣ *ng* at the end of a word, the suffix -*ing* is represented by a light dot—

requesting,	*ordering,*	*meeting,*	*covering,*	*serving,*
assisting,	*attempting,*	*morning,*	*wanting,*	*running.*

The dot *-ing* is used after downward *r* and a light straight down-stroke—

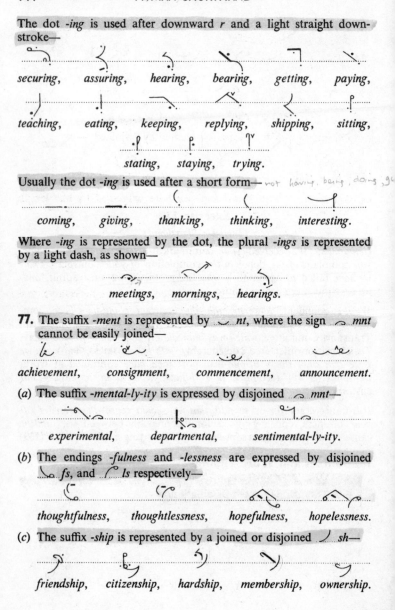

securing,   assuring,   hearing,   bearing,   getting,   paying,

teaching,   eating,   keeping,   replying,   shipping,   sitting,

stating,   staying,   trying.

Usually the dot *-ing* is used after a short form— *not having, being, doing, go*

coming,   giving,   thanking,   thinking,   interesting.

Where *-ing* is represented by the dot, the plural *-ings* is represented by a light dash, as shown—

meetings,   mornings,   hearings.

77. The suffix *-ment* is represented by ‿ *nt*, where the sign ⌒ *mnt* cannot be easily joined—

achievement,   consignment,   commencement,   announcement.

(a) The suffix *-mental-ly-ity* is expressed by disjoined ⌒ *mnt*—

experimental,   departmental,   sentimental-ly-ity.

(b) The endings *-fulness* and *-lessness* are expressed by disjoined ⟍ *fs*, and ⌒ *ls* respectively—

thoughtfulness,   thoughtlessness,   hopefulness,   hopelessness.

(c) The suffix *-ship* is represented by a joined or disjoined ∕ *sh*—

friendship,   citizenship,   hardship,   membership,   ownership.

(d) *-Lity* or *-rity*, preceded by any vowel, is expressed by disjoining the preceding stroke—

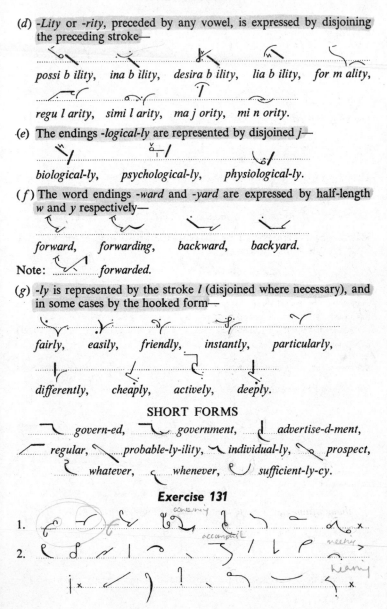

possi b ility,   ina b ility,   desira b ility,   lia b ility,   for m ality,

regu l arity,   simi l arity,   ma j ority,   mi n ority.

(e) The endings *-logical-ly* are represented by disjoined *j*—

biological-ly,   psychological-ly,   physiological-ly.

(f) The word endings *-ward* and *-yard* are expressed by half-length *w* and *y* respectively—

forward,   forwarding,   backward,   backyard.

Note: *forwarded.*

(g) *-ly* is represented by the stroke *l* (disjoined where necessary), and in some cases by the hooked form—

fairly,   easily,   friendly,   instantly,   particularly,

differently,   cheaply,   actively,   deeply.

SHORT FORMS

govern-ed,   government,   advertise-d-ment,   regular,   probable-ly-ility,   individual-ly,   prospect,   whatever,   whenever,   sufficient-ly-cy.

Exercise 131

1.

2.

3.

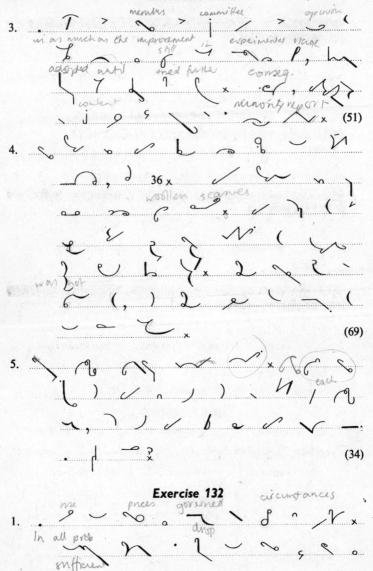

members committee opinion

in as much as the improvement still in experimental stage

adopted until tried further conseq.

content minority report (51)

4. (69)

36 x

woollen scarves

was hot

5. (34)

each

Exercise 132

1.

use prices governed circumstances

In all prob disp

sufficient

report covering   export   import trade issued

2. ⌃ ⌐ — ⌐ — —

annually by the gov't   dept of commerce

Most   ‖ dept stores ‖ ad. reg

3.

whenever

particularly   Christmas, Easter   more

shopping   usual ‖ stores . increase the   of their adverts

. internship   additional

cover   expense   adverts if Evidently   sufficiently profitable

stores continue   campaigns   interruption   Probably

method   estimating   fairly accurately

getting   full   from their ad. campaigns.

In addition   regular news. adverts.

by   direct mail

announcement to indiv   calling their   attention

offerings

(116)

recognising

agree   in the matter of   and adver'tng

cheapness   others   often been instrumental   helping

+ comforting   trying circumstances

(148)

Exercise 134

(Write in Shorthand)

Dear-Sir, *Your*-letter dated *the* 4th reached us *this* morning. *Your instructions have-been* noted, *but-we-are* afraid *that-it*-will-not-*be* possible *to*-make *all-the* alterations contained *in-your* memorandum *and-have-the* book ready *by-the* end *of-this* month. *However,* we fully recognize-*the* desirability *of-having-the* publication completed at *an* early date, *and-we-are* requesting *our* printer *to* hasten-*the* setting *and* printing *as-much-as*-possible.

The inscription will-*be*-placed after-*the* title page, *as you* desire. Proofs *of-the* last chapters will-*be* forwarded *to-you within a* few days.

Announcements will-*be published in next* Saturday's papers *to-the* effect *that a* new novel by *a* prominent *writer* will *shortly* appear. Please *tell*-us if-*you would rather have*-us use *your* name *in-the* announcement. *Very*-truly-*yours,*   (142)

CHAPTER XVII

78. Diphones

Two consecutive vowels, pronounced in two separate syllables, are represented by the angular signs ⌐ ⌐ These signs are called *Diphones*. *✓ ONLY THIS ONE NEED BE USED*

The first ⌐ represents a dot vowel followed by any other vowel, and the second ⌐ represents a dash vowel followed by any other vowel. The signs are written in the place of the first vowel of the combination. *(ONE SIGN WILL DO FOR ANY DIPHONE)*

(1) *payable, saying, carrying, earlier, earliest, idea, ideal,*

material, piano, radio, previous, obvious, premium, medium,

really, real, realize, convenience, convenient, experience,

agreeable, glorious, cordial, courteous, seeing, senior,

serious, studying, theatre, various, Canadian.

(2) *co-operate, co-operation, following, drawing, growing,*

knowing, lower, lowest, poem, showing, accruing, jewel.

79.
The consecutive vowels in words like *question* are represented by the sign ⌐ as in—

question,   union,   suggestion,   million,   guardian.

149

Simpler the outline — the more important the vowel becomes.

80. Medial W

There is a small group of words in which *w* combined with a vowel in the middle of a word is represented by a small semicircle to give an easier or shorter outline. A left semicircle represents *w* followed by a dot vowel, and a right semicircle represents *w* followed by a dash vowel. The semicircles are written in the place of the vowel with which the *w* is combined— *Just use one, if at all.*

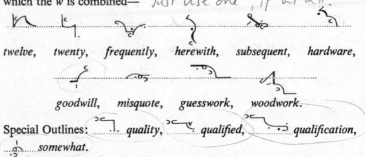

twelve,   twenty,   frequently,   herewith,   subsequent,   hardware,

goodwill,   misquote,   guesswork,   woodwork.

Special Outlines: .... quality, ... qualified, ... qualification,
.... somewhat.

81. Upward SH

The stroke ⟋ *sh* is written upward in certain cases to obtain a better outline—

finish,   shave,   shift,   dash,   fish,   brush,   associate,

association,   appreciate,   appreciated,   appreciation,   foolish,

flash,   shell,   social,   shoulder, etc.

82. Stroke R

To keep the outline close to the line of writing, the upward *r* is generally used where *r* follows two downstrokes. For the same reason, downward *r* is used finally after two straight upstrokes—

prepare,   procedure,   upstairs,   downstairs,   visitor,   despair,

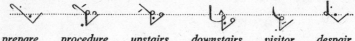

disappear,   treasurer,   furniture,   Shakespeare,   rarer.

83. Stroke S

The stroke *s* is written (*a*) in words like ⌇ *science*, ⌇ *scientific*, ⌇ *sighing*, ⌇ *Siam*, where a triphone immediately follows initial *s*, and (*b*) in words like ⌇ *continuous*, ⌇ *fatuous*, ⌇ *strenuous*, ⌇ *pious*, where the final syllable *-ous* is immediately preceded by a diphthong.

SHORT FORMS

⌇ *danger*, ⌇ *financial-ly*, ⌇ *mortgage-d*, ⌇ *neglect-ed*, ⌇ *practic(s)e-d*, ⌇ *university*, ⌇ *English*, ⌇ *exchange-d*, ⌇ *familiar-ity*, ⌇ *telegram*.

Exercise 135

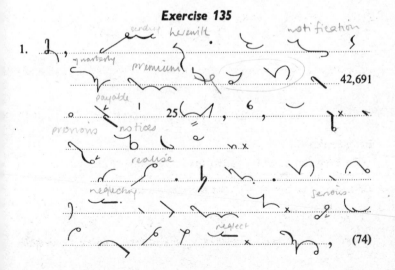

1.   42,691

                                        25   6,

                                              (74)

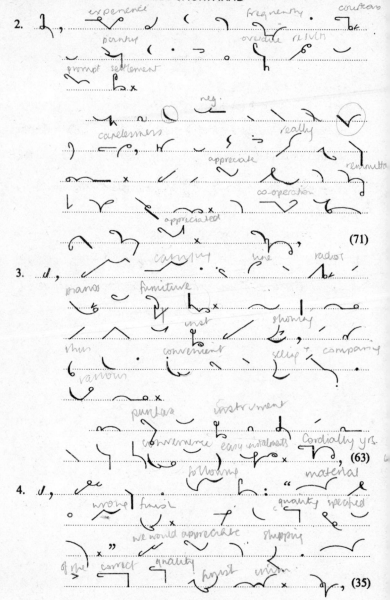

2.

(71)

3.

(63)

4.

(35)

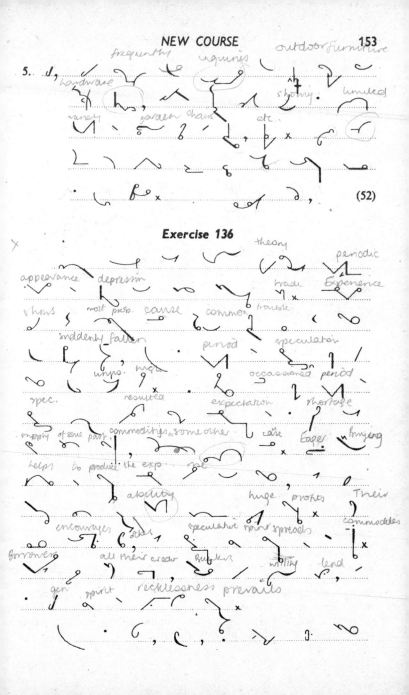

5.

[shorthand outlines with interlinear annotations: frequently, inquiries, outdoor furniture, hardware, showy, limited, variety, garden chairs, etc.]

(52)

Exercise 136

[shorthand with annotations: theory, periodic, appearance, depression, trade, Experience, shows, most prob., cause, common, trouble, suddenly fallen, period, speculators, unpre. mkt., occasioned, period, spec., resulted, expectation, shortage, supply of some park, commodities, some other, case, Eager, buying, helps to produce the exp., ability, huge, profits, Their, encourages, other, speculative, spreads, commodities, Borrowers, all their credit, buyers, willing, lend, gen. spirit, recklessness, prevails]

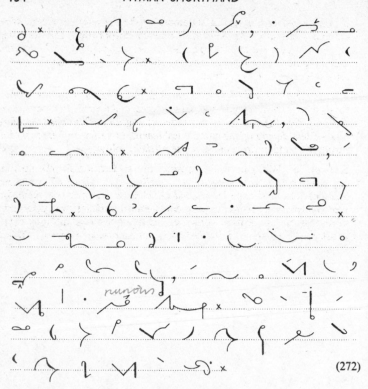

(272)

Exercise 137

(Write in Shorthand)

1. William J. Anderson, *who-is a* professor at Acadia *University, has* recently compiled *a* book *of* quotations *from* Shakespeare. *An* examination *of-the* book shows *that-we-do-*not*-have* to-go *to-the* theatre *to-* hear*-the language of* Shakespeare, *for-we* use *his* terms *and-*phrases constantly *in-our* everyday speech. (53)

2. *We-are* so *familiar with-the-*many conveniences *which* science *has* put *within our* reach *that-we-do-*not realize or appreciate *the* debt *we owe to* science. Constant use *and familiarity with-the* various time-saving *and* labour-saving devices tend *to-*make-*us overlook their* tremendous value. *The* contributions *to-our* comfort *and* convenience by men *of* scientific training *are* continuous, *and-they-have* made*-the* modern world *a wonderful* place *to-*live *in*. (76)

3. *The* treasurer prepares *a* statement *of-the financial* condition *of-the* company annually. *In-the* case *of a public* corporation, *this* statement *is usually sent to-the* stockholders. *A* comparison *with* previous annual reports, or *balance* sheets, shows *whether-the year's trad*ing *has-been more* or less profitable. (48)

4. *It-is-the practice of large insurance* firms *to* invest *the* bulk *of-their* funds *in first mortgages on buildings*, homes, *and* farms. *It-is* considered *that* real estate *is* less liable *to* sudden changes *in* value, *and, therefore, there-is* less *danger of-the* companies' *having to* suffer *any financial* loss through *a* sudden drop *in-the* value *of-their* holdings. (62)

5. *Dear-*Sir, Will-*you* please consider my application *for-the* position *of-*treasurer *in-your organization. I-believe-that I-have-the* necessary qualifications *and* experience, *and-I-*enclose *a* summary *of-them for-your information.* If-*it-is* convenient, *I-shall* appreciate *an opportunity to* discuss my application *with-you, and any* questions *you-*may desire *to* ask *can-be* answered fully *during-the* course *of-our* interview. *Yours-respectfully,* (71)

CHAPTER XVIII

84. Figures

Figures *one* to *seven* and the figure *nine* are best represented by shorthand outlines when they stand alone. Other numbers, except round numbers, are represented by the ordinary arabic numerals. Round numbers are represented as follows—

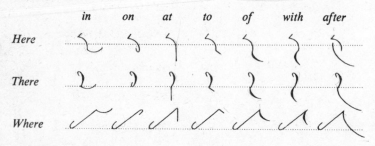

for *hundred* or *hundredth*; 7 700, 2 £200

(or 6 for *thousand*; 5 5,000, 2 £2,000, 3 300,000

for *million*; 4 4,000,000, 2 200,000,000

for *billion*; 2 *two billions*

for *dollar*; 2 *two billion dollars*

85. Compound Words

Compounds of *here*, *there*, *where*, are written as follows—

	in	on	at	to	of	with	after
Here							
There							
Where							

86. Intersections

The practice of intersecting one stroke through another is a very useful device for the representation of very commonly occurring phrases.

The device may be adapted to meet the special needs of the writer. Thus, for some shorthand writers the stroke *p* might usefully represent the word *party*, whereas in an insurance office the stroke *p* might better be used to represent *policy*.

Where intersection is not practicable, write one stroke close to another.
The following list shows how the device may be used—

P represents *party*   Conservative Party

    policy   Insurance policy

B   „   *bank* or *bill*   bank rate

                                               city bank

                                               bill of lading

    business

T   „   *attention*   early attention

D   „   *department*   foreign department

CH   „   *charge*   this charge

    or *charged*   free of charge

J   „   *Journal*   Bankers' Journal

                                               Journal of Commerce

K   „   *company,*   this company
          cover, or
          captain   under separate cover

    capital
    council   Captain Thompson
    kindly

(+S = *experience*)   government official

G + *fvhook* *government*
G   *guarantee*   your guarantee.
G (with *n* hook)
    represents *beginning*   at the beginning

F represents *form*   necessary form

                                               as a matter of form

F with r hook   Firm

TH	represents	*month*		in a month's time
"		*authority* (*-local authority*)		for a month
				next month
S	"	*society*		agricultural society
M	"	*manager,* *morning,* or *mark*		general manager
				Monday morning
				auditor's mark
N	"	*national*		national affairs
		enquiry *insurance*		
L	"	*limited*		Robinson, Limited
RAY	"	*require-d-ment,* or *railway*		you may require
				will be required
				your requirements
				railway officials
R	"	*arrange-d-ment*		please make arrangements
				we have arranged
Kr	"	*corporation,* or *colonel*		public corporation
				Colonel Alexander
Pr	"	*professor*		Professor Jackson
Tr	"	*alternative*		*no ; any*
PL	"	*application*		
Br	"	*branch*		

(annotation: +s)

(margin note: +p 37 notes)

SHORT FORMS

inconvenience-t-ly, distinguish-ed, income, become, becoming, welcome, nevertheless.

Exercise 138

1. 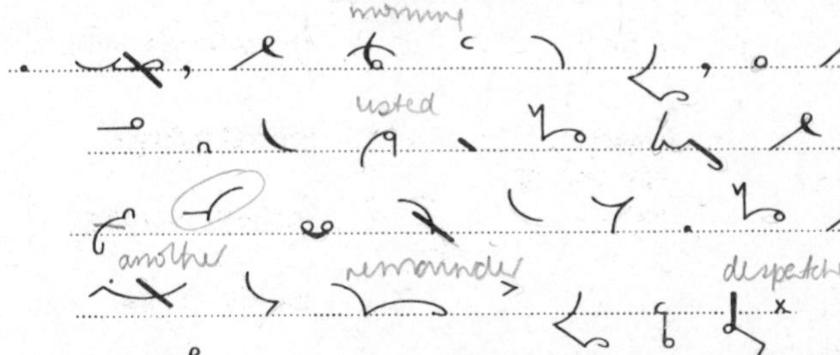

(47)

2. 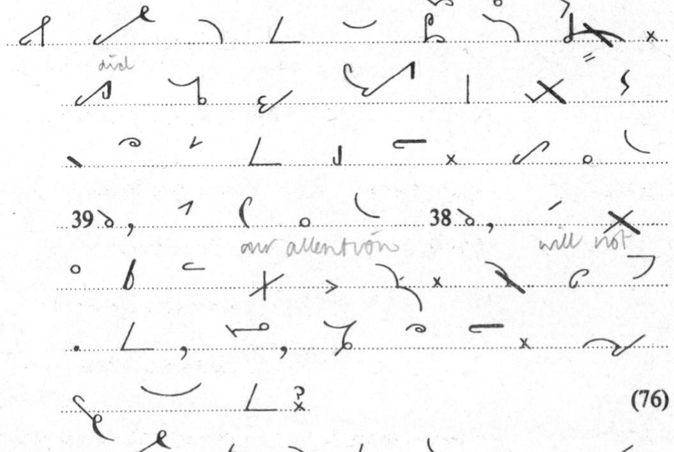

(76)

3. 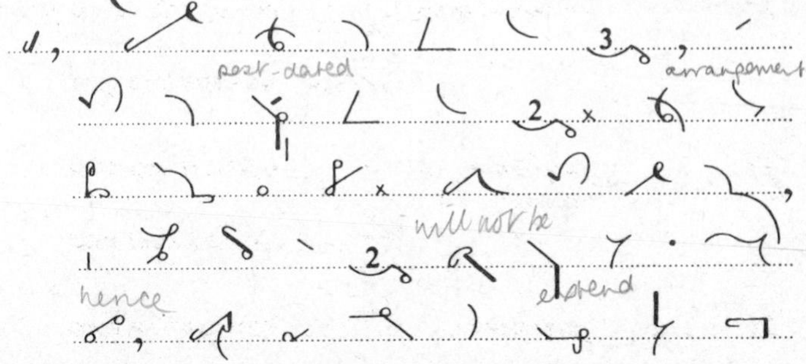

amount

..... 125 .... (shorthand outlines)

ord

..... (shorthand outlines) x

..... (shorthand outlines) Nat. Bank & Trust Co.

..... 125 .... (shorthand outlines)

..... (shorthand outlines) x (shorthand outlines), (122)

4. (shorthand outlines) *need* (shorthand outlines)

..... (shorthand outlines) *requir*

..... (shorthand outlines) ? x

..... (shorthand outlines)

..... (shorthand outlines)

..... (shorthand outlines)

..... (shorthand outlines) *charges*

..... (shorthand outlines)

..... x (shorthand outlines), (89)

Exercise 139

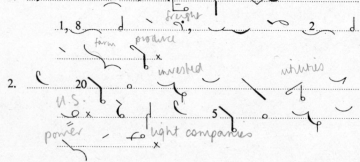

1. (shorthand outlines) 2 (shorthand outlines) *trucks* (shorthand outlines) *trans.* *annually*

1, 8 (shorthand outlines) *freight* (shorthand outlines) 2 (shorthand outlines)

farm produce (shorthand outlines) x

2. (shorthand outlines) 20 (shorthand outlines) *invested* (shorthand outlines) *utilities*

U.S. (shorthand outlines) x (shorthand outlines) 5 (shorthand outlines)

power (shorthand outlines) *light companies* x

3. *(shorthand)* displayished economist aroused attent... political

4. finally arrangements

5. 7(stockholders share dividends declared preferred 40 common 2, 5

6. "Journal" current merge steel iron coc.

7. 6 article recommendation railway commissioners board

8. Treasury Dept Canadian either pol. parties proposed income tax rates

1. Belgium is one of the most densely populated countries in the world within an area of a little more than 11, 5 square miles is confined a pop. of 9, 1

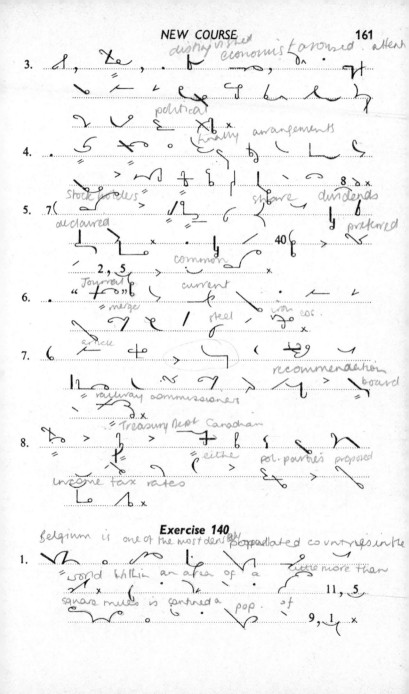

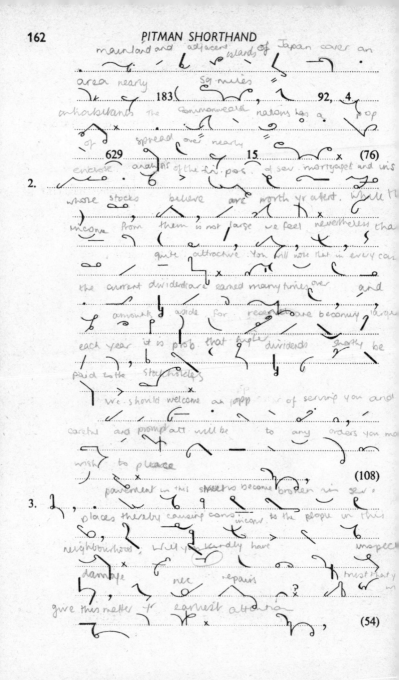

mainland and adjacent islands of Japan cover an area nearly 183(sq miles, 92, 4 inhabitants the Commonwealth nations has a pop of spread over nearly 629 15 x (76)

2. enclose. arah. of the liv. pos. d sev. mortgages and ins whose stocks believe are worth yr attent. While the income from them is not large we feel nevertheless that quite attractive. You will note that in every case the current dividends are earned many times over and amount y aside for reserve are becoming larger each year it is prob. that higher dividends shortly be paid to the stockholders

We should welcome an opp of serving you and careful and prompt att. will be to any orders you may wish to please x (108)

3. pavement in this street is become broken in sev. places thereby causing consid. incon. to the people in this neighbourhood, will you kindly have inspect damage nec repairs must that y give this matter yr earnest attention (54)

Short Forms

LIST ONE

The number in parenthesis indicates the chapter in which the word is presented.

A

a (4)

accord-ing (14)

acknowledge (15)

advantage (12)

advertise-
-ment-d (16)

all (9)

altogether (10)

an (4)

and (6)

any (5)

anything (9)

are (6)

as (8)

as is (9)

B

balance (12)

balanced (12)

be (1)

because (8)

become (18)

becoming (18)

been (12)

behalf (12)

belief (11)

believe-d (11)

beyond (7)

build-ing (11)

but (1)

C

call (11)

called (11)

can (5)

cannot (12)

care (11)

cared (14)

certificate (15)

chair (11)

chaired (14)

character (15)

cheer (11)

cheered (14)

child (14)

circumstance (16)

cold (11)

come (3)

commercial-
-ly (16)

could (10)

D

danger (17)

dear (11)

deliver-y-ed (11)

description (11)

different-ce (5)

difficult (12)

difficulty (12)

distinguish-
-ed (18)

do (1)

doctor, Dr. (11)

during (11)

E

English (17)

equal-ly (11)

equalled (11)

especial-ly (9)

everything (11)

exchange-d (17)

expect-ed (10)

eye (7)

F

familiar-ity (17)

February (10)

financial-ly (17)

first (9)

for (4)

from (11)

G

general-ly (12)

gentleman (12)

gentlemen (12)

give-n (3)

go (5)

gold (12)

govern-ed (16)

government (16)

great (12)

guard (12)

H

had (4)

hand (15)

has (8)

have (2)

he (7)

him (3)

himself (9)

his (8)

hour (6)

how (7)

however (11)

I

I (7)

immediate (15)

important--ce (14)

impossible (14)

improve-d--ment (14)

in (5)

income (18)

inconvenience--t-ly (18)

individual-ly (16)

influence (9)

influenced (9)

inform-ed (10)

information (13)

inscribe-d (16)

inscription (16)

inspect-ed--ion (10)

instruction (16)

instructive (16)

insurance (10)

interest (15)

investigation (13)

is (8)

is as (9)

it (1)

itself (9)

J

January (10)

K

knowledge (15)

L

language (9)

large (6)

largely (11)

larger (11)

largest (9)

liberty (11)

Lord (3)

M

me (7)

member (11)

mere (11)

more (11)

mortgage-d (17)

most (9)

Mr. (11)

much (9)

myself (9)

N

near (11)

neglect-ed (17)

never (10)

nevertheless (18)

New York (9)

next (9)

nor (11)

northern (12)

nothing (9)

November (10)

number-ed (11)

O

object-ed (13)

objection (13)

of (4)

on (4)

opinion (12)

opportunity (14)

organization (13)

organize-d (13)

ought (5)

our (6)

ourselves (9)

over (11)

owe (5)

owing (9)

own (11)

owner (11)

P

particular (14)

people (11)

pleasure (11)

practic(s)e-d (17)

principal-ly (11)

principle (11)

probable-
-ly-ility (16)

prospect (16)

public (13)

publication (13)

publish-ed (13)

put (5)

Q

quite (10)

R

rather (15)

regular (16)

remarkable (11)

remark-ed (11)

remember-
-ed (11)

represent-
-ed (12)

representative
(12)

respect-ed (10)

respectful-
-ly (11)

responsible-
-ility (12)

S

satisfaction (13)

satisfactory (10)

school (15)

schooled (15)

sent (10)

several (8)

shall (2)

short (15)

should (6)

significance (16)

significant (16)		third (12)		welcome (18)	
signify-ied (16)		this (8)		what (7)	
something (9)		those (8)		whatever (16)	
southern (12)		though (9)		when (7)	
speak (8)		thus (8)		whenever (16)	
special-ly (8)		till (11)		whether (14)	
spirit (15)		to (1)		which (1)	
subject-ed (8)		to be (5)		who (1)	
sufficient- -ly-cy (16)		together (10)		whose (6)	
sure (11)		told (12)		why (7)	
surprise (11)		too (1)		wish (5)	
surprised (11)		toward (12)		wished (10)	
		trade (12)		with (7)	
T		tried (12)		within (12)	
telegram (17)		truth (11)		without (10)	
tell (11)		two (1)		wonderful-ly (15)	
thank-ed (6)		**U**		word (15)	
that (10)		under (15)		would (7)	
the (1)		United States (9)		writer (15)	
their (11)		university (17)		**Y**	
them (2)		usual-ly (2)		yard (15)	
themselves (9)		**V**		year (6)	
there (11)		very (11)		yesterday (13)	
therefore (15)		**W**		you (7)	
they are (11)		was (2)		young (9)	
thing (3)		we (3)		your (6)	
think (2)					

Short Forms

LIST TWO

The Short Forms given in the text are for words that are very frequently used. The following additional short forms will be found useful in high-speed writing. The words occur in lists of the ten thousand commonest words.

A

administrator

appointment

arbitrary

arbitration

architect-ure-al

assignment

B

bankruptcy

C

capable

characteristic

contentment

D

dangerous

defective

deficient-ly-cy

demonstrate

demonstration

destruction

discharge-d

E

efficient-ly-cy

electric

electrical

electricity

emergency

England

enlarge

enlargement

entertainment

enthusiastic-m

establish-ed-ment

executive

executor

expediency

expenditure

expensive

I

identical

identification

imperfect-ion-ly

incorporated

independent-ly-ce

indispensable-ly

influential-ly

intelligence

intelligent-ly

introduction

investment

irregular

J

jurisdiction

justification

L

legislative

legislature

M

manufacture-d

manufacturer

manuscript

mathematics

maximum

mechanical-ly

messenger

minimum

ministry

misfortune

monstrous

N

negligence

notwithstanding

O

objectionable

objective

P

passenger

peculiar-ity

perform-ed

performance

practicable

prejudice-d-ial-ly

preliminary

production

productive

project-ed

proportion-ed

prospective		stranger	
publisher		subscribe-d	
		subscription	
Q		substantial-ly	
questionable-ly		suspect-ed	
		sympathetic	
R		**T**	
reform-ed			
remarkable-ly		telegraphic	
representation		thankful	
republic			
republican		**U**	
respective		unanimous-ly	
respectively		uniform-ity-ly	
		universal	
S		universe	
selfish-ness		**V**	
sensible-ly-ility		valuation	

Short Forms

LIST THREE

The following Short Forms do not occur in lists of the ten thousand commonest words.

A

abandonment

administratrix

amalgamate

amalgamation

arbitrate

arbitrator

attainment

C

circumstantial

contingency

cross-examination

cross-examine-d

D

denomination-al

destructive

destructively

E

enlarger

enlightenment

executrix

exigency

extinguish-ed

F

falsification

familiarization

familiarize

G

generalization

H

henceforward

howsoever

I

imperturbable

inconsiderate

informer

intelligible-ly

irrecoverable-ly

irremovable-ly

irrespective

irrespectively		remonstrance	
irresponsible-ility		remonstrate	
M		removable	
		reproduction	
magnetic-ism		retrospect	
mathematical-ly		retrospection	
mathematician		retrospective	
metropolitan		**S**	
O		signification	
obstruction		stringency	
obstructive		subjection	
oneself		subjective	
organizer		**T**	
P		thenceforward	
performer		**U**	
perpendicular			
perspective		unanimity	
proficient-ly-cy		universality	
proportionate-ly		unprincipled	
prospectus		**W**	
R		whensoever	
recoverable		whereinsoever	
reformer		wheresoever	
relinquish-ed		whithersoever	

INDEX

References are to the paragraph numbers unless otherwise stated

FURTHER PITMAN NEW ERA SHORTHAND BOOKS

THE PITMAN DICTIONARY OF ENGLISH AND SHORTHAND
This 928-page indispensable work of reference contains words with clear concise definitions and fully-vocalised shorthand outlines written in position, as well as an excellent introduction containing more than 1500 shorthand outlines to exemplify rules.

A NEW REVIEW OF PITMAN SHORTHAND
Assuming a complete coverage of the theory in the *New Course*, the 15 chapters of this book contain theory, short forms and phrasing, followed by a wealth of interesting application material. Each chapter concludes with business correspondence concerning a single company so that continuity is maintained.

THE NEW PHONOGRAPHIC PHRASE BOOK
A valuable comprehensive course in phrasing for those who have already studied a basic textbook.

THROUGH PRACTICE TO PRODUCTION
This book contains extensive reading and dictation material on the short forms, phrases and theory linked to the *New Course* and combines dictation, transcription, typewriting and English to assist the student in achieving the integration of shorthand and typewriting skills.

PITMAN NEW ERA SHORTHAND SPEEDBUILDER
Providing a thorough revision of short forms and main phrasing principles, *Speedbuilder* contains a wide range of commercial correspondence, and timing columns to enable the students to measure their own progress.

LEARNING AND TESTING SHORT FORMS
Graded with the *New Course*, each chapter lists the short forms introduced in the *New Course* and, after the third chapter, continues with (a) sentences in shorthand for reading and writing practice, (b) sentences in longhand for conversion into shorthand, and (c) ten-word sentences for dictation practice.

PITMAN SHORTHAND SPEED DEVELOPMENT NO 3
A selection from the RSA Single Subject Examination Papers 1966–1969 (50–120 w.p.m.), counted for dictation together with a shorthand key.

PRE-RECORDED DICTATION MATERIAL

A NEW REVIEW OF PITMAN SHORTHAND

Six $3\frac{3}{4}$ i.p.s. tapes providing dictation of the two long shorthand passages and the business correspondence contained in each chapter of *A New Review of Pitman Shorthand* and dictated at 70 and 90 w.p.m.

PITMAN SHORTHAND SPEED DEVELOPMENT NO 3

Five $3\frac{3}{4}$ i.p.s. tapes or ten C60 cassettes containing timed dictation of all the material in the corresponding book. Each passage is dictated twice, the first dictation being at the examination speed and the second dictation at a higher speed.

SPEEDON CASSETTES

Each cassette contains four passages, each of four minutes duration, dictated first at the basic speed and repeated 10 w.p.m. faster. The material on Cassette 1 is dictated at speeds from 50–80 w.p.m. and that on Cassette 2 is recorded at speeds from 90–120 w.p.m. A leaflet with the New Era Key is available on request.

PITMAN NEW ERA FRENCH SHORTHAND DICTATION

Five tapes or five C60 cassettes containing timed dictation of all the practice material contained in the corresponding book, plus two additional passages, dictated at speeds ranging from 50 w.p.m. to 110 w.p.m.